Landscape Archaeology

Landscape Archaeology

*An Introduction to Fieldwork Techniques
on Post-Roman Landscapes*

Michael Aston BA and
Trevor Rowley BA   BLitt   FSA

DAVID & CHARLES
Newton Abbot   London   Vancouver

0 7153 6670 X
LOC 74-83302

© Michael Aston and Trevor Rowley 1974

All rights reserved. No part of this publication may be reproduced, stored in a retrieval system, or transmitted, in any form or by any means, electronic, mechanical, photocopying, recording or otherwise, without the prior permission of David & Charles (Holdings) Limited

Set in 11 on 13pt Garamond and printed in Great Britain by Latimer Trend & Company Ltd Plymouth for David & Charles (Holdings) Limited South Devon House Newton Abbot Devon

Published in Canada by Douglas David & Charles Limited 3645 McKechnie Drive West Vancouver BC

Contents

List of Illustrations 7
Introduction 11

CHAPTER 1   LANDSCAPE ARCHAEOLOGY   13
The antiquarian tradition · Medieval landscapes · The nature of landscape fieldwork

CHAPTER 2   TECHNIQUES OF FIELDWORK   28
Land ownership · Basic equipment · Fieldwalking · The recording of earthworks · Linear earthworks · Fieldwork in built-up areas · Buildings · Place-names · Questionnaires · Production of finished plans and maps

CHAPTER 3   MAPS AND LANDSCAPE ARCHAEOLOGY   56
Cartographic evidence · Estate maps · Enclosure and tithe maps · Ordnance Survey maps

CHAPTER 4   AERIAL PHOTOGRAPHY   75
Earthworks · Townscapes · Cropmarks · Soil marks · Plotting cropmarks and earthworks on to maps · Sources of aerial photographs

CHAPTER 5   FIELDWORK IN TOWNS   90
The site · Town plan · Buildings · Names

CHAPTER 6   FIELDWORK IN VILLAGES   117
The village plan · Buildings

CHAPTER 7   FIELDWORK IN THE COUNTRYSIDE   131
Deserted towns and villages · Medieval agriculture · Castles · Moated farmsteads · Fishponds and mill sites ·

Medieval parks · Linear earthworks · Monastic sites · Fields and hedges · Medieval industry · Roads and bridges

CHAPTER 8 THE ORGANISATION AND APPLICATION OF FIELDWORK 165
Card indexes · Maps · Photographs · A Sites and Monuments Record · The M40 Archaeological Research Group · Recording sites in Redditch New Town, Worcestershire · Publication

Notes and References 182

Appendices
1. *Victoria County History* published volumes 194
2. Royal Commission on Ancient and Historical Monuments published volumes 195
3. Brunskill building recording form and cards 196
4. Medieval Village Research Group fieldwork questionnaire 198
5. Moated Sites Research Group introduction to field card 201
6. Oxford City and County Museum primary record card 204
7. Essex County Council archaeological record 205
8. Ordnance Survey conventions for site recording 206

Bibliography 208

Acknowledgements 210

Index 211

List of Illustrations

PLATES

Old Sarum, Wiltshire	17
Abergavenny, Monmouthshire	17
Worton, Oxfordshire	18
Middleton Stoney, Oxfordshire	18
Totnes, Devon	35
Bentley, Essex	36
Little Wittenham, Berkshire	36
Cricklade, Wiltshire	85
Ludlow, Shropshire	86
Warwick	103
Wantage, Berkshire	103
Old Radnor, Radnorshire	104
Merton, Oxfordshire	104
Castle Acre, Norfolk	153
Newbold Grounds, Catesby, Northamptonshire	153
Halton, Northumberland	154
Somerton, Oxfordshire	171
Abberwick, Northumberland	171
Sawley Abbey, West Riding, Yorkshire	172

MAPS AND PLANS

1. Kilpeck Castle, Herefordshire, and Burwell Castle, Cambridgeshire   22

List of Illustrations

2	Cassington, Oxfordshire	38
3	Washford, Redditch, Worcestershire	40
4	Hachure plan of a hypothetical site	41
5	Comparison of an earthwork feature and its hachure plan	44
6	Laying out a right-angled triangle	45
7	Offset measurements in planning earthworks	46
8	Coordinate measurements in planning earthworks	47
9	Contour surveying on a grid with level and staff	47
10	Composite plane table and level surveying	48
11	Alvechurch, Worcestershire, Feckenham Park, Hanbury, Worcestershire	58
12	Milton under Wychwood, Oxfordshire	61
13	Bosvenning, Roskennal and Bodinnar, Sancreed, Cornwall	62
14	Atcham, Shropshire	63
15	Rousham, Oxfordshire	65
16	Boarstall, Buckinghamshire	67
17	Halesowen, Worcestershire	68
18	Diagram of shadows and highlights, soil marks and cropmarks	78
19	Drayton, Berkshire	87
20	Haverfordwest and Liverpool	93
21	Malmesbury, Wiltshire	94
22	Richard's Castle, Herefordshire	95
23	Warwick	96
24	Oxford Region	98
25	Bristol and Lincoln	98
26	Hereford	100
27	Wallingford, Berkshire, and Oxford	101
28	Northampton and Southampton, Hampshire	102
29	Stratford-upon-Avon and Thame	105
30	Flint and Caernarvon	108
31	Worcester and Durham	112
32	Pontefract, Ely and Castle Rising	116
33	Castle settlements in Shropshire	120

34	Nuneham Courtenay and Marsh Baldon, Oxfordshire	121
35	Church plans	125
36	Enstone parish, Oxfordshire, and parishes in south Warwickshire	134
37	Ducklington, Oxfordshire	135
38	Castle Camps, Cambridgeshire	136
39	Wormleighton, Warwickshire and Lower Dornford, Wootton, Oxfordshire	138
40	Castle Acre, Norfolk, and Clare, Suffolk	141
41	Shrunken villages in Oxfordshire	142
42	Kenilworth Castle, Warwickshire	147
43	Midland moated sites	150
44	Moated sites in Tanworth and Ullenhall parishes, Warwickshire	151
45	Fishpond sites in the Midlands	152
46	Bordesley Abbey, Redditch, Worcestershire	156
47	Medieval parks	158
48	Maxstoke Priory, Warwickshire	160
49	Plans of post-medieval formal garden earthworks	163
50	Archaeology and the M40 motorway	176
51	Redditch New Town, Worcestershire	177

Introduction

Despite an increasing volume of literature covering landscape archaeology, there is little printed practical advice available, either for the novice or for those students wishing to further their studies. As archaeological excavation becomes increasingly specialised and professionally controlled, the authors feel it is appropriate for the part-time enthusiast who wishes to make an original contribution to the subject to turn increasingly to fieldwork. It is with this hope in mind that our book has been designed to help stimulate and guide senior school, extra-mural, college and undergraduate studies of post-Roman landscapes in England and Wales. When we look at the countryside today, we see at one glance a compendium of ingredients. It is the task of the landscape archaeologist to recognise, to record and to understand the various elements.

This book also attempts to forge a link between field archaeology, which has a long and honourable tradition in this country, and the infant study of landscape history. It does not, however, attempt to present a comprehensive survey of what is an enormous and diffuse subject. Here we offer a modest manual of fieldwork techniques which can be employed by individuals or groups working on areas and topics of their own choice. It must be stressed that evidence of man's past activity in this country is so extensive that there is no region where such work will be wasted. Time and again areas which at first sight appear archaeologically and historically barren have turned out to be of the greatest interest when examined in detail. This has been well demonstrated by fieldwork carried out ahead of

Introduction

motorway construction, where large numbers of previously unidentified archaeological sites have been discovered in areas at first thought to be archaeologically bare (Fig 50).[1] The implication of these discoveries is that estimates of Romano-British, Anglo-Saxon and medieval populations in the past have been far too low.

We are both geographers by training and feel that the geographical approach has still much to contribute to the study of landscape history. While we would not wish to become involved in the discussions concerning the value and validity of the statistical approach of the 'new geography' and the 'new archaeology', we do feel that our job is to encourage the collection of information through fieldwork. Scholars in the future may have the leisure to analyse and synthesise, but at the moment we are all in the front line as far as rescuing a representative sample of our field archaeology is concerned. Our historical landscape is under threat, and we hope that our book will help fieldworkers to record and understand the countryside before large parts of it have gone for ever.

M.A. and T.R.

The reference to this Introduction is given on p 182

CHAPTER I

Landscape Archaeology

Prehistoric landscapes have received much attention in the past, particularly in those upland areas where they are best preserved. It has been argued, however, that the very survival of such early features in an upland context is in itself misleading. They may reflect marginal activities in areas which have always been marginal; it is quite possible that the equivalent contemporary information reflecting lowland activity has been lost as a result of subsequent occupation, cultivation and mineral extraction. For example, on the Berkshire Downs large but diminishing areas of prehistoric earthworks survive, while on the adjacent gravels of the Upper Thames Valley, all surface trace of equally dense archaeological material has been ploughed out, and is now visible only from the air as cropmarkings (Fig 19).

None the less, while there is undoubtedly room for still more intensive fieldwork on prehistoric and Romano-British landscapes, this book is principally concerned with the period from the departure of the Romans to the beginning of the Industrial Revolution. This includes all those earthworks and landscape features dating from the migration, Anglo-Saxon and medieval periods. Large areas of the English countryside are covered with earthworks dating from these periods. The fact that these earthworks are now fast disappearing makes the need to record them all the more important and urgent.

Landscape history has belatedly begun to feature in the environmental discussion, and with our greater awareness of countryside and townscape as sources of historical information, the need to recognise the significance of features and the ability to record them has become increasingly important. Change occurs in our modern landscape at such a dramatic rate that the need to record has never been greater. Urban redevelopment and expansion, mineral extraction, new towns, motorways and the removal of hedgerows to create larger fields, all take their toll of the historical environment. Many of the features with which we are concerned are individually small, but together they constitute an important whole. We are at last developing a national conscience about, for instance, the felling of trees, because we recognise that such beautiful objects take decades to grow and cannot quickly or easily be replaced. We should develop a similar conscience about the destruction of our landscape – its hedges, fields, tracks and buildings – which can never be replaced. Justifiable concern has been expressed about the obliteration of archaeological sites and individual historic buildings without looking at them first; the argument should now be extended to include the whole historical environment. This is irreplaceable and should not disappear before it has been at least observed and charted. We would not passively watch the destruction of medieval documents; just because our ancient landscapes are not encapsulated in libraries or archives, it should not deter us from protesting when they are threatened.

The landscape is a palimpsest on to which each generation inscribes its own impressions and removes some of the marks of earlier generations. Constructions of one age are often overlain, modified or erased by the work of another. The present patchwork nature of settlement and patterns of agriculture has evolved as a result of thousands of years of human endeavour, producing a landscape which possesses not only a beauty associated with long and slow development, but an inexhaustible store of information about many kinds of human activities in the past. The landscape archaeologist needs to develop an eye and a feeling for patterns in town and country and, even more important, to recognise anomalies in, for instance, the large isolated medieval church of the deserted medieval village; the straight stretch of stream channelled by monks in the

Landscape Archaeology

thirteenth century; the regular eighteenth-century Parliamentary enclosure hedge lying across medieval ridge and furrow; the lumpy ground next to the church, marking the site of an old settlement; and even a fine Jacobean building in an otherwise apparently poor area, indicating a former prosperity linked to a long-forgotten trade or industry. Ideally it should be possible to look at any feature in the landscape, know why it is there in that form, and understand its relation to other features. This approach has been well expounded by Beresford and Hoskins (see p 19), but the features to look for and how to record them are perhaps not understood so well.

Our towns, villages, roads and fields are, to a greater or lesser extent, all relict features from earlier periods. All are expressions of economic, social and political forces that have disappeared or at least been considerably modified. If we look at any medieval provincial town in England, we shall almost certainly find that the central street pattern was laid out in the Middle Ages. It is, therefore, little wonder that the motor car and our ancient towns are so often in conflict with each other. During the period of medieval town plantation, roads were often diverted to pass through the middle of towns in order to attract trade and tolls (Figs 24 and 29). Ironically, many of our modern by-passes are required because traffic enticed into towns by speculative planning some seven centuries ago is no longer welcome in the narrow and winding streets created for a very different system of transport.

Essentially the landscape reflects the past. Even a contemporary new town has an element of obsolescence. It might be 20 years on the drawing-board and a further 20 in the building and, by the time the town is completed, it may be almost half a century out of date in design and concept. The canal geography of the eighteenth century and railway geography of nineteenth-century Britain are important reminders of how technology can change the landscape.

THE ANTIQUARIAN TRADITION

The tradition of observing and recording field monuments in Britain dates back to at least the Middle Ages. Medieval historians such as Giraldus Cambrensis, Geoffrey of Monmouth and William of Malmesbury often referred to archaeological sites and monuments in their writings.[1]

A recent example of the value of such information was provided by the excavation of the Greyfriars Church, Oxford, which William of Worcester had visited and paced in 1480.[2] This church must have been one of the most impressive structures in medieval Oxford, and William's dimensions, including a north nave which he recorded as containing ten chapels, seemed inexplicable until confirmatory evidence was archaeologically excavated.

Thus the works of such notables as the great topographer John Leland (1503-52), William Camden (1551-1623), John Aubrey (1626-97) and William Stukeley (1687-1765), have become sources in their own right. We read and quote them, not for the interpretation of the evidence, which is frequently wildly wrong, but because of the record they provide of archaeological sites and monuments in the past. Unfortunately not all of their work has been published. For instance, Aubrey's survey and record of archaeological sites, the *Monumenta Britannica*, is still available only in manuscript form.[3] The *Monumenta* attempted to describe in detail a selection of field monuments from prehistoric times to the Middle Ages throughout the country, and includes sketch plans of monuments such as the Iron Age and medieval defences at Old Sarum, Wiltshire (see plate, p 17).

Apart from these well known topographers, much local field archaeology was recorded by county historians and topographers, who were particularly active during the eighteenth and nineteenth centuries. More often than not the field archaeologist is irritated by the scholarly writing of these men working exclusively from documentary sources and oblivious to plan or shape of settlement, building or earthworks. Occasionally, however, they do make a valuable reference to a monument or building and sometimes even oblige with a plan. Sir William Dugdale drew a series of county maps to accompany his *Antiquities of Warwickshire* (1756), and on these he marked deserted villages with a special symbol. Robert Plot (1646-96) in his *Natural History of Oxfordshire* (1677) described several sites in the county, including ornamental waterworks at Enstone, which have since been demolished without trace. Field evidence often turns

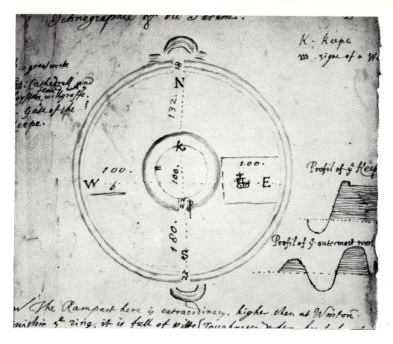

Page 17 (above) *Old Sarum, Wiltshire. John Aubrey's plan made in the seventeenth century. It shows the site of the Cathedral, and profiles of the prehistoric earthwork defences and the central Norman castle;* (below) *Abergavenny, Monmouthshire. Sir Richard Colt-Hoare's plan of the town in the late eighteenth century. It shows clearly the castle, the priory, and the line of the medieval town wall (which has now largely disappeared)*

Page 18 (above) *Worton, Oxfordshire.* Ploughed-out ridge and furrow visible at ground level as soil marks. The light areas mark the stony ridges, while the furrows filled with top-soil show up as darker lines; (below) *Middleton Stoney, Oxfordshire.* An estate map of 1737 showing the old manor house with a possible cruck gable. The medieval church, now rebuilt, and the earthen motte of the Norman castle are characteristically represented in an eighteenth-century prospective style. The village was moved to the edge of an extended park in the early nineteenth century

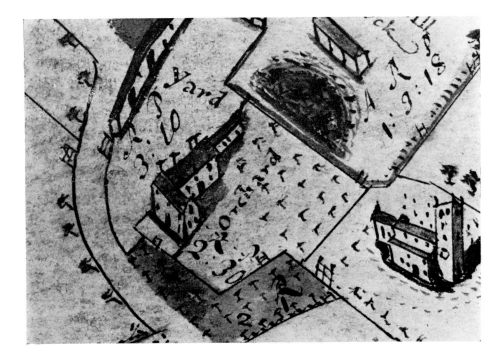

up in unlikely places: for example, the great civil engineer, Thomas Telford (1757–1834) recorded some archaeological monuments in great detail,[4] and Sir Richard Colt-Hoare (1758–1838), better known for his rural fieldwork and excavations, produced a number of plans of medieval towns, such as Abergavenny (see plate, p 17). In this century the fieldworking technique has been continued by such notables as O. G. S. Crawford and L. V. Grinsell.

A comprehensive history of the closely allied study of British field archaeology is contained in Paul Ashbee's paper 'Field Archaeology: its origins and development'.[5] However, the work of Prof Maurice Beresford, whose *History on the Ground* (1957) consists of a series of detailed case studies, must be recorded here. Earlier his *Lost Villages of England* (1954) heralded a new era in the study of the medieval landscape, providing an immense stimulus to work on settlement studies and medieval archaeology. His most graphic work on the subject, produced in collaboration with Prof J. K. S. St Joseph, was *Medieval England: An Aerial Survey* (1958). This book, regrettably now out of print, contains an impressive collection of photographs of medieval sites and monuments, providing the only extensive survey of the English medieval landscape.[6] Prof Beresford later opened up another extremely rich area of landscape studies with his *New Towns of the Middle Ages* (1967).

The modern pioneer of landscape studies is, however, Prof W. G. Hoskins. 'Despite the multitude of books about English landscape and scenery, and the flood of topographical books in general, there is not one book which deals with the historical evolution of the landscape as we know it.' This was his assertion at the very beginning of his now classic book *The Making of the English Landscape*, published almost 20 years ago in 1955. This book has been followed by a series of county volumes.[7] Quite apart from large numbers of papers on aspects of landscape history, Prof Hoskins later wrote two books of particular interest to the landscape historian – *Local History in England* (1959) and *Fieldwork in Local History* (1967).

In this brief history of the subject reference should be made to the Ordnance Survey's *Field Archaeology: Some Notes for Beginners*, first published as long ago as 1921. A revised edition appeared in 1963 and there was a further revision in 1973. The author of the first volume was O. G. S. Crawford, whose *Archaeology in the Field* (1953) has long been regarded as a major contribution to British field archaeology. Another useful introduction to British field monuments is *Collins Field Guide to Archaeology in Britain* by Eric S. Wood (1963), which contains a considerable amount of sound information; however, much of it is concerned with prehistoric monuments, a feature common to such guides.

Recently there have been a number of publications specifically dealing with landscape history. The Council for British Archaeology has published papers given at a conference on field archaeology in Britain,[8] and *Archaeology and the Landscape, Essays for L. V. Grinsell*, edited by Peter Fowler, was published in 1972. This contained a series of important papers on the role and nature of fieldwork. Reference should also be made here to the 'Discovering' series of booklets, which deal with a variety of landscape topics, often providing a valuable introduction to aspects of landscape study.[9]

For most areas, the only available survey of the field monuments will be contained in the relevant county volume of the *Victoria County History* (see Appendix 1). Archaeological material normally appears in Volume I, together with the geographical, geological and botanical background and the transcript of the Domesday Book (1086). Since many of these volumes were compiled earlier this century, the earthwork plans are sometimes inaccurate and often completely inadequate. These surveys were associated with the work of the Earthworks Committee of the Congress of Archaeological Societies, which was effectively formed in 1907. A 'Provisional Scheme' and a 'Hint for Helpers' were issued and the classification these set out was used by the compilers of the *Victoria County Histories*. The original aim was to produce an accurate archaeological survey of each county – a laudable objective, but one which is sadly still far from being achieved.

The Royal Commission on Ancient and Historical Monuments TRCAHM), founded in 1908, also works mainly on a county basis The Commissions for England, Scotland and Wales are separate organisations, but each is required by Royal Warrant to 'prepare an

Inventory of the Ancient and Historical Monuments and Constructions connected with or illustrative of the culture, civilisation and conditions of life of the people of the relevant county from the earliest times, and to specify those which seem most worthy of preservation'. Eventually the Commission will produce a complete historical gazetteer, but of necessity it works painstakingly slowly, and it is more than likely that by the time it begins to study many areas, much information will already have been destroyed (see Appendix 2). Also, despite a broadening of its approach in recent years, the Commission is still largely concerned with individual buildings or monuments and not with the total historic environment. Nevertheless it is interesting to compare the different approaches evident between an earthwork plan of Kilpeck (Hereford) produced in the 1930s and one of Burwell Castle (Cambridge) produced in the 1970s (Fig 1).

MEDIEVAL LANDSCAPES

The earthworks and cropmarks recording man's activities in the Middle Ages are no less characteristic than those of prehistoric times. Until recently archaeologists paid comparatively little attention to the earthworks of medieval England. Medieval archaeology has suffered to some extent from the conservatism of settlement in the last 1,000 years. It is the misfortune of medieval archaeology that successive generations have so seldom quarrelled with the original choice of site. In any medieval village which has become a town the sites of cottages and crofts have been covered with houses and shops, and the density of modern settlement and the high values of urban land have offered little opportunity for excavation. Only excavation before redevelopment sometimes reveals the village beneath the town.

Villages which have not expanded into towns have been all the more conservative in their siting. The evidence of maps from the sixteenth century onwards suggests that the general direction of streets and the relative position of the house and garden units have often changed little over the last 400 years, and probably not for some centuries earlier, but the ideal site for fieldwork is one where

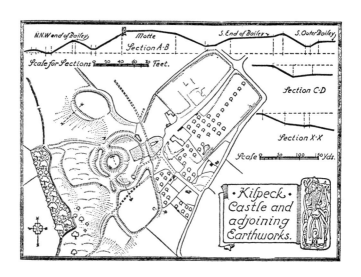

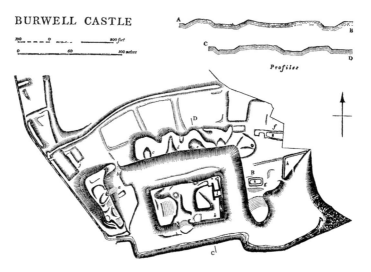

Fig 1 Kilpeck Castle, Herefordshire (1931–4): large motte and bailey castle with adjacent deserted medieval village enclosure. Burwell Castle, Cambridgeshire (1972): unfinished castle earthworks overlying deserted Saxo-Norman village earthworks. Plans by Royal Commission on Ancient and Historical Monuments

later modifying influences have been weak. The village or town abandoned before the Great Rebuilding,[10] the medieval port choked by silt, the borough which wilted soon after its first plantation, the market town 'fossilised' by a diversion of routes – these offer the best examples of medieval topography. There have been comparatively few surveys concerned exclusively with post-Roman antiquities,[11] and while we would not wish to divorce these elements from fieldwork on sites of earlier periods, we believe that their neglect in the past has been unfortunate, particularly in view of the current rate and scale of landscape change.

THE NATURE OF LANDSCAPE FIELDWORK

Landscape fieldwork basically involves observing and recording mainly relict features with the aim of explaining the evolution of patterns and shapes in urban and rural landscapes. This means not only the examination and survey of those sites and earthworks of obvious archaeological interest, but also examining the form of towns and villages, the shapes of fields and the alignment of tracks and boundaries. It also requires the interpretation of surviving visible features in a parish or region, and especially the inter-relation between these features. A complete manual on the necessary techniques for total landscape understanding would, however, consist of many volumes. Here we are simply suggesting techniques for observing and recording archaeological and historical elements in the landscape. One of the delights of this approach is that it is essentially non-destructive, and a considerable amount of evidence can be quickly collected. Unlike an excavation, a piece of landscape fieldwork is open to repetition, reappraisal or modification, and most of the evidence normally remains available for reassessment.

One word of warning at the very outset: it would be naïve and arrogant in the extreme to believe that landscape archaeology holds all the answers to the past. We are suggesting ways of looking at the landscape, since our main aim is to help record, and we also put forward ways of understanding and interpreting. The fieldworker must be content to submit possible reasons for the shape and alignment of the features he examines, but he cannot possibly work in a vacuum. In later chapters ways are indicated in which the fieldworker may cooperate with documentary historians and workers employing more traditional forms of archaeological techniques. Indeed, if one is to fully understand the landscape, one needs a combination of all possible disciplines. Such an approach has been called 'total archaeology' but 'landscape history' or 'landscape archaeology' would possibly be more apt, for they incorporate all aspects of the natural and man-made landscape and their relations.[12] We cannot pretend that it is an easy task, and the fieldworker may well find refuge in some esoteric specialisation. The successful landscape archaeologist needs to be a 'jack of all trades', part geographer, botanist, archaeologist and historian as well as possessing some elementary knowledge of engineering techniques, to understand, for instance, how mills function and how and why buildings are constructed in such different ways.

Primarily the fieldworker requires an ability to appreciate the countryside in all its forms. This is certainly the most difficult job of all. Most of us, by training or inclination, see certain aspects of the landscape but not others. Each member of a group of specialists walking across a piece of country sees a somewhat different landscape. The field geologist, by observing changes in soil colour and texture, may be able to identify differences in soil types and divisions between drift geological deposits. The botanist will recognise plants that may indicate former areas of marsh. The geomorphologist can see a line of low rounded gravel knolls that is a small moraine deposited under or just in front of an ice sheet, and where Roman engineers, medieval peasants and twentieth-century construction gangs may have dug for building and road materials. The prehistorian recognises struck flint flakes that show him where earlier people lived, while the medieval archaeologist notices traces of ridge and furrow indicating where medieval and later farmers cultivated their fields. The vernacular architectural historian will recognise the plan of a late-medieval house even though it is entirely encased in nineteenth-century brick, and the art historian quickly sees architectural characteristics in an eighteenth-century house indicating the work of a particular designer. Only patience and practice will give the fieldworker an appreciation of all these skills, though he can soon develop an eye for patterns and features of particular interest.

One of the principal justifications for recording the landscape is that, despite a fine tradition of archaeological fieldwork in Britain, the landscape itself has for too long been ignored. It may seem quite extraordinary to us today, but one can open any economic history textbook written before World War II and find no reference to deserted medieval villages. The immense social and economic implications of the abandonment of settlements, which was countrywide, and the subsequent movement of population are only now filtering into the textbooks. How many other major historic factors manifest themselves in the landscape but remain to be identified? Perhaps nothing quite on the scale of deserted villages, but we are confident that there are many unseen or underestimated aspects in the landscape remaining to be recognised and recorded. The art historian would not dream of writing about the development of architectural styles without closely examining the physical evidence of the buildings; similarly historians cannot write about past communities without analysing the shape, form and function of their settlements. To some extent the documents tell us what earlier peoples thought with their minds, but what did they construct with their hands?

Thus, simply as a source of information, landscape studies are justifiable and necessary. We need to build up comprehensive regional archaeological distribution maps. It is now a truism that all archaeological distribution maps are inaccurate, recording only those limited areas where fieldwork has been carried out in the past. We need to have a much more complete picture of, for example, the distribution of moated sites or fishponds than we do at the present time. Only the compilation of detailed gazetteers will enable us to understand changing patterns of settlement and land use.

The destruction of archaeological sites is a twofold problem, involving on the one hand the increasing rate of destruction of known sites, and on the other the identification of a considerable number of previously unknown sites just before or at the time of their destruction. There can be little doubt that this is by far the greatest problem facing British archaeology at the moment.[13] Field archaeology can help in two ways: firstly by identifying the sites before destruction, and secondly by providing some form of record of those sites which cannot be excavated.

In order to formulate excavation priorities, we need many more detailed local studies. The nature and rate of redevelopment means that it is impossible to excavate all threatened sites. If we are to make rational decisions about which are the most important sites or which are likely to yield the most information, we need to have an intimate picture of a locality. Excavation is becoming increasingly costly and time-consuming, and in order to make the most effective use of limited archaeological resources we need a programme of local, regional and eventually national priorities. Some readers may find these sentiments disquieting; bureaucracy is something archaeology can well do without, but we must face the fact that we are undertaking major programmes of excavation with a minimum of background (fieldwork) data. The nature of the threat is too serious to be treated in such a cavalier manner.

On a smaller scale, when faced with an extensive earthwork site, the archaeologist should have a detailed ground plan with all the associated information at his disposal in order that he can make decisions about where to place his cuttings. Here the field archaeologist can provide much of the basic data on which decisions on excavation policy may be based. Frequently, only the nucleus of a castle or monastic site will have been identified or properly surveyed;[14] by completing the picture with the details of earthworks of outlying buildings and boundaries the field archaeologist will be giving a fuller picture of the site, as well as putting it in its local context (Figs 46 and 48 and plate, p 172).

At the same time there is a very strong case to be made for the preservation of areas of landscape – town, village and countryside – in order that representative samples may be kept for closer analysis in the future. Most of our totally inadequate ancient monuments' legislation is aimed at the conservation of single buildings or archaeological sites. We need to look at whole areas and to isolate certain sections as landscape parks – a hedge-line which is ten centuries old deserves attention in the same way as other archaeological antiquities. It is to be hoped that the current interest in field archaeology will help in the location and recording of landscape features and provide a basis for selective preservation, perhaps eventually leading to effective legislation for the protection of site and landscape.

Notes and references to this chapter begin on p 183.

CHAPTER 2

Techniques of Fieldwork

Fieldwork, unlike archaeological excavation, can be undertaken either by individuals or groups. Projects carried out by small groups can be particularly rewarding, since the different viewpoints and interests of each person can throw light on features which may be only superficially recorded or even missed by an individual, and at the same time relatively large areas of ground can be quickly covered. This fieldwork may take the form of, for example, a regional survey of early parks or ridge and furrow, or it may constitute part of a national scheme on the identification and recording of deserted medieval villages or moated sites. The work may contribute to an archaeological rescue scheme – along the line of a motorway, over an area to be covered by a new or expanding town, or on an area of threatened river gravels – or it may be undertaken simply for reasons of academic research. Fieldwork can also take the form of recording monuments or areas to assess, such as the state of preservation of scheduled sites. Little systematic fieldwork has been undertaken in Britain in the past, in contrast to other areas of northern Europe, and this is one of the reasons why the density of archaeological sites revealed by redevelopment has come as something of a surprise.

The time involved in a fieldwork project will vary considerably. A brief survey of a field for pottery and other artefacts may take a few minutes, a complete sketch plan can take several hours, and a detailed survey of a region may take months. Whatever the nature and scale of the exercise, the fieldworker should clearly define the area of his interest at the very beginning. In this type of research there is always a real danger of wasting time and energy by pursuing too many lines of inquiry.

LAND OWNERSHIP

It is absolutely essential to obtain permission from the owner or tenant before walking over fields or entering premises. The fieldworker should explain the reasons for his interest, as this will reassure the owner and often prompt farmers or tenants to volunteer valuable information about an area or site. If there is any difficulty in finding out the farmer's name, the regional office of the National Farmers' Union may be able to help.

Certain information about land ownership and tenantry is useful in anticipating threats to archaeological sites by ploughing or levelling, although its personal nature demands considerable tact in its gathering. Not all the information may be readily obtainable. In rural areas a threat is most likely to arise with a change of ownership bringing in a tenant with different ideas of farm management, or a new landlord intending to make heavy investment in new buildings or extensive improvement of land. The acquisition of an area by a mineral extraction company poses an obvious and large-scale threat to any archaeological evidence. When dealing with a large-scale redevelopment, it is important to determine at what stage the developer is to acquire the land. Sometimes the land will not change hands until within a few weeks of redevelopment starting. Accordingly, along the line of a proposed motorway, for instance, it may be necessary to approach dozens of different farmers in order to obtain permission to fieldwalk the route in advance of construction.

BASIC EQUIPMENT

With practice the fieldworker will soon find out what minimum equipment he requires for his particular task, bearing in mind that when working he has to carry most of it about with him. A drawing board, a piece of formica or hardboard of at least A4 size, clips, notebook, paper (plain or graph) or tracing film, pencils and rubbers represent the basic equipment. A set of coloured pencils can be useful when there are a variety of features to be recorded.

The OS 1in (1: 63,360) or new 1: 50,000 map should always be available, and the appropriate map of the area, usually an OS 2½in (1: 25,000) map should also be carried. This is the smallest scale map on which many topographical features such as field boundaries are shown. The OS 6in (1: 10,560) is usually necessary for detailed field and village surveys. (As part of the metrication programme the 1in and 6in maps are currently being replaced by 1: 50,000 and 1: 10,000 sheets.) Sometimes, especially in towns, the OS 25in (1: 2,500) map is essential. A prismatic compass may be required for taking bearings, particularly in featureless areas. A 5, 10 or 15m tape will normally be needed, as well as a shorter hand tape. More elaborate surveying equipment will generally only be required for specific recording exercises.

A camera is an indispensable memory aid and means of recording, as well as providing illustrative material for publication and teaching. All the photographs taken with the date, name of site, viewpoint, grid reference and direction of view, should be recorded, either separately on a list or on the plans produced at the same time. Photographs should be taken from several viewpoints, especially in low light. Ideally the fieldworker should use a 35mm single-lens reflex camera for monochrome photographs, with a similar second camera for colour transparencies if possible, but any photographic record is better than none at all. A ranging pole to indicate scale is useful, preferably one which can be dismantled and easily carried. The fieldworker should also carry polythene bags in which to collect sherds of pottery (paper bags disintegrate when wet), as well as slips of paper or card to record the location of finds. It is important for the fieldworker to keep a notebook to record his activities, visits and observations. Features of apparent insignificance recorded initially may become important as work progresses.

FIELDWALKING

One of the most effective techniques of collecting archaeological information is by fieldwalking. The best time to walk is immediately after ploughing in the autumn or spring, but information can be gathered in all seasons, and ideally a field should be seen under a variety of different conditions, even those areas under permanent pasture. Several visits may be necessary, and the fieldworker should remember that he sees only part of the evidence at any one time: for instance, in different seasons the amount of visible surface information will vary considerably. The fieldworker should also be aware of the differential survival of evidence: hard-fired and glazed pottery is likely to survive for longer in a surface context than less resistant pottery which has been tempered with grass or grog (broken-up pottery fragments). A spread of worked flints without associated pottery may simply mean that the pottery which was originally there has been weathered away. The absence of significant surface pottery in fields where cropmarks have been identified need not deter the fieldworker from looking for other forms of surface evidence.

The fieldwalker should always be aware, when collecting evidence, that all surface finds are unstratified and not in an archaeological context. This is particularly important to remember in the case of isolated sherds or coins, which may just have found their way into a field by way of a cart of manure rather than from an underlying archaeological site.

Apart from collecting surface information, the fieldworker should take advantage of any surface disturbances such as road-widening or pipe-laying schemes. Often these will provide valuable archaeological evidence in the form of sections, as well as any artefacts which may come to light. Whatever the nature of the finds made during fieldwalking, further exploration through excavation by untrained fieldworkers should be discouraged. Archaeological excavation is a highly specialised technique and should be undertaken only by competent archaeologists.

A detailed knowledge of local drift geology and soils will help considerably, and when working in a new area, it will probably take some time to adapt to new regional conditions. The Ordnance Survey publishes a series of solid and drift geological maps for the Institute of Geological Sciences, as well as soil survey maps.[1] The Stationery Office also publishes a series of regional geological surveys, though it is far from complete. Consideration of the geomorphological features may also be useful,[2] as it may be doubtful whether some features are natural or man-made. For example, large slabs of oolitic limestone are to be found all over north Oxfordshire, either incorporated in prehistoric burial chambers or lying in a natural position looking remarkably like structural remains.[3] In such cases the fieldworker should simply record his observations. In certain regions stone slabs were traditionally used for roofing.[4] The mapping of areas over which a particular type of stone is used in wall building and roofing materials can provide valuable information,[5] and there are some good local surveys of building materials which may be consulted.[6]

Flint and stone

When man took to fashioning stone tools he soon discovered that tough fine-grained rocks provided the most suitable material. They are capable of forming strong cutting edges and points, and since they break with a fairly regular and dependable fracture, they lend themselves to shaping better than do softer and coarser rocks. Flint is found in layers in the upper chalk, either in slabs or in nodules.

In some areas where flint occurs naturally, it may be some time before implements are located. Many natural formations look remarkably like worked flint and, conversely, irregular chunks or flakes may prove to be whole implements or parts of them. If tools have worked edges or 'secondary working', this usually needs to be proved, calling for either a detailed knowledge of flints or recourse to an expert.[7] Any flint found in an otherwise flint-free area will obviously be significant, although it may have been transported there recently. The same is true of any stone material foreign to the area being examined, and instances of this should be recorded on the fieldworker's map and in his notebook with appropriate comments.

Implements were also made of stone, the best known being the polished stone axes of Neolithic times. Quartzite pebbles, polished on one side, can come from the mould-boards of ancient ploughs. Sharpening and grinding stones are frequently found. Complete querns and millstones, or parts of them, are to be found not only in farmyards and next to mills but in hedgerows and sometimes built into stone walls. Sandstone rubbers and sharpening stones, often cigar-shaped, can be picked up in fields; most are post-medieval.

Iron
Ironwork such as nails, rings, old ploughshares and miscellaneous pieces of farm machinery found in ploughed fields may well be of recent origin. Hand-made forged nails only ceased to be made in the early nineteenth century. Normally such ironwork is of little value in archaeological or landscape terms. Iron tools of antiquity may be encountered throughout Britain, but if they have been on the surface for any length of time, they are likely to be heavily corroded. However, spreads of iron slag or clinker, as it is generally known, can be important for the identification of possible ironworking or industrial sites.

Non-ferrous metals
Although coins, bronzes and even gold and silver finds are occasionally made, their value to the landscape historian is normally limited. The metal may indicate an abandoned site or just the casual loss of an object. In any case the search for coins or precious metals should be discouraged. The widespread use of metal detectors for this purpose in recent years has led to the indiscriminate pillaging of some sites, and the removal of such objects from their archaeological context must be deplored.

Burnt clay
This can frequently be found in ploughed fields where there has been earlier occupation. It can be red, cream or grey-black and sometimes has impressions of finger or twig marks from its original function as part of a wattle and daub building. Clay furnishes more valuable evidence when found in association with other archaeological material such as pottery, where it may indicate a buried kiln site, or, in association with charcoal, possibly the remnants of domestic buildings which have been destroyed by fire.

Bricks and tiles
Spreads of bricks, tile and mortar may indicate the site of a building

of Romano-British, medieval or post-medieval date, or even the production centre for these materials. Often, however, they simply represent dumps of hard-core for field entrances or at gates between fields, or the ploughed-out remains of drives or yards. In some cases vitrified bricks may indicate kiln sites. Knowledge of the date of the first use of brick in any area will help with the interpretation of the site, and a particularly valuable exercise is to try to build up a local chronology of bricks and tile types. Brickmaking died out after the Romans left, and was reintroduced from the Low Countries in the early thirteenth century. These were large bricks $10\frac{1}{2}$–12in × 5–6in × $1\frac{3}{4}$–$2\frac{3}{4}$in, but later a series of smaller bricks was introduced. Until the sixteenth century, however, there was no recognised standard, and even then there remained a great deal of variety. The present size is generally 9 × $4\frac{1}{2}$ × 3in. One may encounter a considerable variety of Roman tiles, ranging from those used in a heating system to roofing tiles. Roman tiles were often re-used in churches and houses before the reintroduction of bricks. Individual pieces of mosaic floor known as tesserae, which are frequently in the form of small coloured stones, may also be found, although it is unlikely that they will occur without other evidence. Medieval floor and wall tiles are often decorated or glazed and can normally be readily distinguished from ordinary roofing tiles.[8] Tiles were extensively used for roofing again from the sixteenth century onwards.

Pottery
Pieces of pottery, known as sherds, are the most important artefacts to look for during fieldwalking, and their distribution should be plotted in some detail. The discovery of a spread of pottery, together with other evidence of occupation such as bones, mortar and tiles, may lead to the identification of a previously unknown archaeological site. The fieldworker should notice whether the sherds are cleanly broken or are worn and abraded, the latter indicating prolonged rolling about in the plough soil. A considerable number of wasters (misshapen pot fragments) found in association with burnt daub could indicate a kiln site. Approximate areas of buried occupation sites as indicated by spreads of pottery can be marked out on a plan

Page 35 *Totnes, Devon. Vertical air view*, with the medieval burgage plots, castle and lines of town defences highlighted by low sunlight and contrasting with more recent development

Page 36
(above) *Bentley, Essex.* Oblique air view of cropmarks, some of which reflect medieval settlement and agricultural features while others represent natural periglacial frost cracks. Notice how a different crop to the north does not register cropmarks as clearly;
(below) *Little Wittenham Berkshire.* Oblique air view of ploughed-out ridge and furrow appearing as dark and light bands, apparently cutting across a series of underlying rectangular features of uncertain date

for future reference. Domestic pottery up to the Middle Ages was usually very coarse and black, grey or red in colour, but in most periods there have been better wares. The variety of fabrics and forms increases throughout the Middle Ages.

The fieldworker should acquaint himself with the colours, fabrics and textures of the prehistoric, Romano-British, Anglo-Saxon and medieval pottery likely to be encountered in the area he is surveying. This can most readily be done by visiting local museums and if possible handling material in the reserve collections. It is worth remembering, however, that dirty broken fragments of pottery found in the field will look very different from complete vessels in a museum.

Soil colours

Concentrations of charcoal or very black soil can relate to an underlying occupation or early industrial site. Large circular patches may, however, represent the legacy of itinerant industrial activity such as charcoal burning. Soil colours may also help in deciding the extent of sites affected by ploughing. Spreads of darker material may show ditch sites or rich humic material over occupation areas, while light soil or stony patches may indicate ploughed-out banks or mounds. A ploughed-out example of ridge and furrow amply demonstrates the dark lines of the old furrows, and the lighter drier, stonier and often less fertile lines of the ridges (see plate, p 18).

Glass

Glass varies in colour with its age and composition. Roman glass is tinted green, brown or yellow, with vivid iridescence. Saxon glass found in south-east England tends to be clearer and whiter. From the mid-thirteenth century glassmakers used potash and the glass is mostly greenish. Fragments of decorated glass may be found near churches or monasteries.

All the above observations should be plotted on to 6in or 25in OS maps, with their approximate positions marked. When collecting pottery, it may be necessary to divide the field into quadrants or strips, using a tape and ranging rods or bamboo canes, and then systematically to collect artefacts over these smaller areas. Fig 2 illustrates the results of an exercise of this nature carried out on a gravel area at Cassington (Oxon) where there was a marked relation between the densest distribution of pottery and the cropmarks identified from aerial photographs. All surface finds should be gently cleaned and marked in Indian ink with the find-spot, date and initials, using white ink if the object is dark. Coins and other unmarkable objects should be kept in small envelopes or containers. Local museums, archaeological societies or public libraries are always pleased to hear of surface finds.

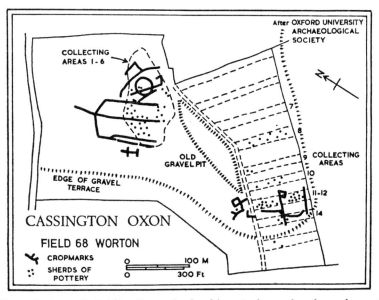

Fig 2 Cassington, Oxfordshire. Cropmarks plotted from air photographs and areas demarcated for pottery collection after ploughing. There is a close correlation between scatters of Romano-British potsherds and the cropmarks, probably indicating the existence of one or more Romano-British farmsteads

THE RECORDING OF EARTHWORKS

Sketch planning
The normal way to record earthworks is to employ one of the con-

ventional surveying techniques,[9] but this may not always be possible. A substitute for detailed survey is sketch planning, a method applicable to a variety of different sites. Many of the plans in this book were prepared by this method. This technique, though limited, is particularly valuable when carrying out a rapid field reconnaissance. It also has the advantage of requiring little equipment, only a drawing board, paper, pencils and a rubber. The results of sketch planning may even be more informative than a contour plan. Fig 3 shows the same area of earthworks at Washford, Worcestershire, depicted by both techniques.

Although many earthwork forms are easily recognisable, others are not so well defined. The fields of low rounded indeterminate humps and hollows which are frequently found in the Midlands and North may represent a deserted medieval village, an abandoned drainage or irrigation system, or a group of shallow worked-out marl-pits. A sketch plan will often help to distinguish between the possibilities. Apart from summarising the broad outlines of the relations within any individual site, sketch planning is an important tool in field reconnaissance over a wide area. A considerable number of site plans can be produced quickly for assessment and comparison.

The basic method of producing a sketch plan can be summarised as follows:

> (a) The fieldworker should walk over all parts of the site to see how extensive it is and assess the most prominent or important features found there.
>
> (b) He should then draw the large, well defined features or those of high relief first, and avoid concentrating in too much detail on any one part of the site to begin with. Only when the main features have been drawn and the relations between them recorded as accurately as possible should the smaller details be added.
>
> (c) As drawing progresses, notes and sketches should be made of boundaries, roads and buildings, so that the finished product can easily be related to the 6in or larger-scale OS maps. Constant objects such as buildings or large trees should be employed

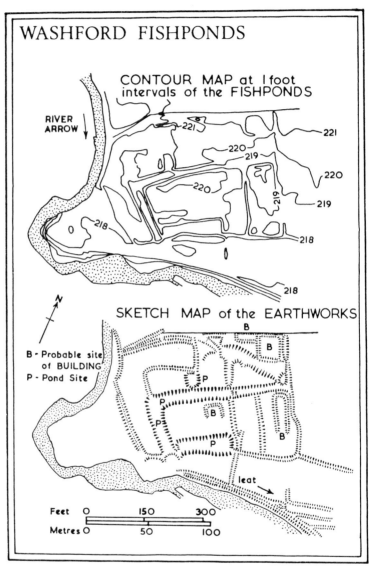

Fig 3 Washford, Redditch, Worcestershire. Plan of the fishponds, now destroyed, depicted by contour lines and hachures. It will be noted that even with contour intervals of 1ft much of the detail is still not revealed

as base-line features, with the neighbouring buildings, field boundaries and field corners being used as reference points.

(d) Final corrections should be made after a further walk over the site to ensure that the finished plan accurately represents the features on the ground.

(e) Lastly a fair copy of the plan should be drawn, using hachures to depict changes of slope.

To help illustrate this technique let us take a hypothetical field with low-relief earthworks lying close to a parish church which the fieldworker is visiting (Fig 4). As far as he knows, these earthworks

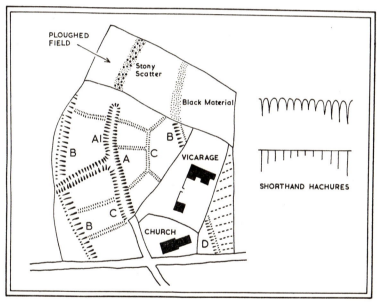

Fig 4   Hachure plan of a hypothetical earthwork site

have not been recognised or recorded in any way. He may know little or nothing of the history or archaeology of the area and have no information other than the earthworks themselves on which to base an interpretation. Similarly it is probable that he will not know whether the site is likely to be ploughed, built over, quarried away or otherwise destroyed in the near future. Finally he may have only an hour to spare. Under these circumstances he should attempt to draw a sketch plan, even if he has only the back of an envelope on which to work.

Having obtained the farmer's permission, one's first task is to walk all over the site up to the field boundaries, continually looking at it from different angles in order to assess the approximate shape and main features of the area, and to find out whether the site extends beyond the present enclosure. Close attention should be paid to field boundaries and adjacent properties. In Fig 4 the field to the north has been ploughed, but there are surface patches of stone and black humic material whose distribution will need to be noted. The facts that the modern road ends abruptly on the south-east side of the field and that the field itself is a rather curious shape are also relevant. Having carried out this preliminary reconnaissance and become acquainted with the general layout of the earthworks, the fieldworker can now begin work on his sketch map.

The most prominent features appear to be two large hollows (A) meeting near the centre of the site and reaching the field boundaries at two points. The first operation should be to plot these hollows, since as soon as they are on paper, all subsequent planning will be easier. It should be noted that one of the trenches runs from the present road's abrupt termination towards a point about one-third of the way eastwards along the northern boundary of the field, with an apparently curved course. Closer examination will reveal that there is a distinct bend in the main trench at A1 and that it does not quite reach the northern field boundary, so that the arc-like features first drawn will have to be slightly amended. The position of the other trench can now be placed in relation to the first one, since it meets it about half-way along, and on a line between the north-east corner of the field and a point just over half-way down the western field boundary. The minor changes in width and depth of these features can then be sketched. Smaller features such as the change of slope at B can be recorded in the same way, and then the areas of minor importance (C) plotted with a reasonable degree of accuracy within the framework of the larger features already positioned, much as one would plot within the grid or triangulation of an orthodox survey.

Throughout the survey the fieldworker should be moving about the site so that each feature can be seen in its complete context. If all the plotting is carried out from one spot or from one side of the site alone, the result will inevitably be distorted.

At this stage the rough sketch map should consist of a number of lines or shorthand hachures and notes of approximate estimated height and length measurements, the latter best expressed in relative rather than absolute terms, eg 'about half-way along field boundary' rather than 'about 10m from corner'. The surrounding fields should then be examined in case they contain features which might help explain aspects of the sketched earthwork. In Fig 4 the features in the ploughed field to the north mirror the banks and ditches within the earthworks in the first field, and this correlation may help with interpretation. Similarly, in the field D south-east of the church and vicarage, a minor earthwork, which in isolation might signify little, is seen to fit into the general pattern of the earthworks over a wider area and should be recorded.

There are various methods of depicting relief, including the use of parallel and perimeter lines with terms such as 'bank', 'ditch', 'mound', or 'hollow' written in. This system, however, lacks flexibility, and it is usually preferable to produce a shorthand version of the hachures which will go on the final plan, and which are capable of equal variation (Fig 4). If the fieldworker chooses the first alternative, the final plan should be drawn up while his memory of the site is still fresh.

Hachures have been a cartographic device since at least the eighteenth century and were used to portray relief on early Ordnance Survey maps. An examination of hachure plans will reveal that a wide range of types of symbol have been employed in the past. The only universal convention applied to hachuring is that the head of the hachure always represents the top of the slope while the tail points downhill. Further standardisation is desirable if plans are to be compared. Variation in the shape of the head may be used to indicate abrupt changes or breaks of slope – a rounded head or *tadpole* showing a gradual change and an angular flat-topped head or *tintack* representing a sharply defined break. Hachures close together represent a steep slope, those farther apart a more gentle one. Generally, heavier hachures are used to reflect the more impressive features on the ground (Fig 5). The hachure length is always related to the length

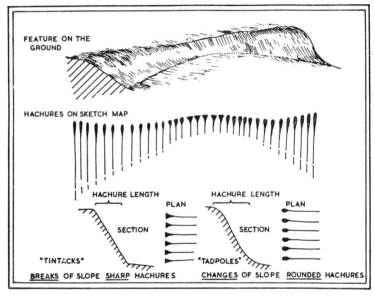

Fig 5 Comparison of an earthwork feature and its hachure plan; suggested conventions for the use of hachures

of the slope in plan and does not depict the steepness of the slope. A variety of instruments can be used to draw hachures – technical pens (rapidographs), brushes, quill pens or even ballpoint pens, but the best results are obtained from an ordinary mapping pen. By variations in pressure and length of stroke, different effects can be achieved and a whole range of slope types expressed. All the hachure plans included in this book have been drawn with an ordinary mapping pen.

It is important to distinguish the man-made slopes from the geological variations of the ground surface. If the site lies on a steep slope, any attempt to show this by means of hachures would only confuse the plan. Natural slopes are best indicated by other techniques, such as a labelled arrow pointing downhill or a few sketched contour or form lines. When plotting man-made features, it is best to consider the natural ground surface as theoretically flat *but not level*, and to show any archaeological features as projecting from this plane surface or excavated into it.

The hachuring should show the magnitude of the various ground features in such a way that on any plan the closest concentration of hachures should reflect the most prominent slopes. Any sketch plan should by this token be correct in its relations within itself.

An alternative but more lengthy method of producing a hachure plan involves the establishment of a grid over the area to be surveyed. This can be done by first laying a base-line, at intervals of say 5m, through the central part of the earthworks or between two points which can be related to the OS map. Alternatively, if there is a straight field boundary, the base-line can extend along this. Bamboo canes provide satisfactory markers; they should have pieces of masking tape attached to them in order that they can be numbered.

The next task is to establish grid squares over the area to be surveyed. This is best done by creating a right-angle, using two or three tapes to make a 3, 4, 5 (Pythagoras) right-angled triangle, and extending the lines from there (Fig 6). There will inevitably be some degree of error in using this technique, but provided that the right-angles and length of each side of the grid square are constantly checked during the layout, the error should remain within an acceptable margin.

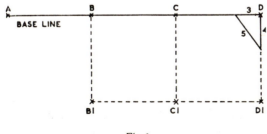

Fig 6

Having laid out the grid, one can begin plotting breaks of slope. This can be done in two ways. Firstly, take right-angled *offset* measurements at regular or strategic intervals from a tape laid down one side of a grid square (Fig 7). Measurements to the top and bottom

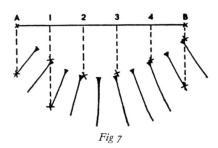

Fig 7

of slopes can then be marked on to a sheet of graph paper. These points are joined together and hachures depicting the slope are then added. The second method involves the use of two tapes anchored either at two corners of the grid squares or anywhere along the perimeter of a square. The tapes are extended and brought together at the point of slope break and thus *coordinated*. These points can be marked on the graph paper by using compasses, but a quicker way is to pin the ends of two narrow pieces of graph paper to the base points and then manipulate them until they give the correct co-ordinate. This method is particularly useful when applied to complicated surfaces (Fig 8).

Both these methods can provide a valuable exercise for beginners, as they involve the fieldworker in making decisions about where breaks of slope start and end. It can also be usefully employed by larger numbers of students, who can be divided up into groups, each of which can be allocated a set of grid squares. Problems frequently arise when the sheets of graph paper are joined together, as the drawings rarely coincide exactly, but this in itself can help illustrate the different interpretation of earthworks. When drawing up a final copy, such discrepancies can be rectified.

Techniques of Fieldwork

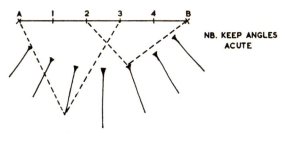

Fig 8

Contour surveys
Ideally the fieldworker should be able to produce a contour survey with 0·50m or 1m intervals. Provided that one of the team is familiar with the use of a level, this need not be a long process. The survey can be conducted in two ways. In the first method the area to be surveyed is staked out in relation to the National Grid, with a grid network at 1, 2 or 5m intervals. Readings can then be taken at the required intervals of say 0·50m. Provided that the level is set up at a convenient point, the staff can be moved easily and readings quickly recorded. Contour lines can then be drawn to join areas of similar height (Fig 9). In the second method, if there is already an accurate hachure plan of the site, the staff can be moved about without the use of a grid and points of identical height marked on and later joined together. A combination of hachures to show man-made features and contours to show natural slopes can produce an

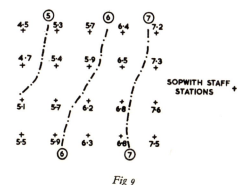

Fig 9

47

Techniques of Fieldwork

acceptable compromise. In all cases it will be necessary to relate the readings to the National Datum. This is best done by locating the nearest bench-mark, often to be found on a church or public building such as the post office or school. The precise imperial and metric height of bench-marks can be obtained for a small fee by writing to the Ordnance Survey.[10]

Composite earthworks survey
The following plane tabling method can be used to produce both a break of slope and contour plan. Three plane tables should be set up along a known base-line. Attached to one table is a sheet of graph paper, and on the other two are placed sheets of tracing paper (ideally these should be sheets of plastic film). Each board is aligned on the base-line and a common scale is adopted for all plans. For each point selected by the staff man in the field a line is drawn by the people at the plane tables. At the end of the survey each of the plans has a series of lines radiating from the point representing the position of the board on the ground. In order to make a map of the points selected in the field, the transparent sheets are placed over the opaque sheet and the base-line and base points aligned directly over each other. The intersection of the radials on the opaque sheet below and the transparent sheets above can then be marked on the upper sheet and the result is, as in the case of conventional plane tabling, a set of points related in angle and distance from the known base-line (Fig 10).

This method of plane tabling uses three boards instead of one, so that the position of the boards after each set of readings remains unaltered. The staff man moves about the field, making it unnecessary

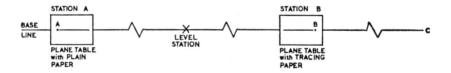

Fig 10

48

to have either a large number of ranging rods or canes in use or frequent movements backwards and forwards for the single board. Three boards are best, for then discrepancies can be detected by any triangles of error formed.

While the plane tabling is being carried out, a level survey can be conducted, readings being taken concurrently. The position of the level does not need to be related to the position of the plane tables, but it is necessary for the staff to be visible at all times from all plane tables and the level station. In practice the level is usually placed between the plane tables, although if it is resited around the field, no particular difficulties in correlation need occur, provided that the staff can be seen by all workers. The field stations are numbered on each plane table map and also against each level reading, so that in drawing up the plans both the relative position and the height of each point are known. It is thus possible to construct a contour plan as well as a plan of the breaks of slope on the same map.

The selection of field stations is most important. The points need to be only roughly positioned at 5m intervals so that the general topography is mapped. The more obvious features, such as linear earthworks, banks and ditches, are plotted in as well as the background grid. The great advantage of this method is that the director can decide on significant points which need plotting as well as conducting the survey of the general grid depicting the slopes of the site. Five or six people are needed for this work – one person on each of the plane tables, one person on the level, one person on the staff and a director (if the staff man is not directing the survey).

When the survey is completed, the fieldworker may be able to make some guesses as to the meaning of his plan; however, as with all interpretations based solely on above-ground evidence, he must form only a working hypothesis. If excavation occurs, it will undoubtedly provide a far more complicated picture. The fieldworker must avoid the arrogance of believing that his interpretation is necessarily the right one or, indeed, that he is doing any more than providing a valuable framework within which archaelogical priorities can be decided.

Let us expand this theme slightly. On any earthwork site, but particularly sites of deserted medieval villages, the features may appear to form a homogeneous structure. However, excavation has repeatedly demonstrated that villages were rarely completely abandoned at one time, and that apparently contemporary earthworks may represent buildings that were deserted over a period of one or more centuries. The earthwork plan of Wharram Percy (E. Riding)[11] shows the early extent of the settlement, with the twelfth-century manor house close to the church; while to the north the thirteenth-century planned village extension, with the new site for the manorial complex, can be seen. Excavation has demonstrated that many of the house platforms represent half a dozen or more different phases of building. At Seacourt (Berks) excavations demonstrated precisely the same phenomenon, but this could not have been predicted from the rather vague but apparently uniform earthworks.[12]

LINEAR EARTHWORKS

Linear banks and ditches form a separate category of earthworks (see p 158), the classic study on them being Sir Cyril Fox's *Offa's Dyke* (1955). There still remains a wide range of major and minor linear earthworks of the post-Roman period worthy of detailed examination. The main principles which should be borne in mind are that such earthworks should be studied in relation to (a) the geological character and relief of the countryside through which they pass, and (b) other known antiquities in the area. An abbreviated and slightly amended version of Fox's scheme for the survey of Offa's Dyke is included below.[13] This technique may also be applied to roads and tracks, whose study has proved particularly popular as a fieldwork exercise.[14]

1 *Introduction.* This should give a brief description of the earthwork and the part and nature of the country through which it passes.
2 *The course of the earthwork.* The course and character of the earthwork should then be described in detail, field by field or stretch by stretch, throughout its whole length, with comments which may need later elaboration. The descrip-

tion is in sections, each illustrated by a strip of the OS 6in map on which to record the nature of the earthwork and other relevant matters.

3 *The existing profile of the earthwork.* A series of level sections spread over the whole length of the earthwork should be taken with a level, a full-sized staff being used to avoid frequent resetting of the instrument. The profiles are then described and analysed.

4 *Passage-ways through the earthwork.* Original openings with rounded (undamaged) ends should be carefully recorded, as should obvious later gaps.

5 *Major and minor alignments.* The term 'alignment' in connection with a linear earthwork has a dual significance. The major alignment is concerned with the plan and general layout in relation to the main features of the country, and may consist of stretches of earthwork often many miles in length, terminated by a definite change of direction and appearing particularly straight on a small-scale map. The minor alignment considers the mode in which the course is set out and the earthwork constructed from point to point within the directional limits thus determined. Variations from a straight to a winding course can readily be classified, plotted, and their significance considered.

6 *Construction.* Variations in the physical form of the earthwork may reflect the employment of different gangs of builders. With this information the fieldworker is equipped to interpret the earthwork in the light of all the other documentary and archaeological evidence available.

FIELDWORK IN BUILT-UP AREAS

Many of our smaller towns and villages have been neglected in the past by fieldworkers. This is unfortunate as there is obviously much that can be learnt from detailed ground survey. The large-scale OS maps showing individual properties and buildings make it easy to walk round a settlement marking on relevant features. The frequency of reference points in towns and villages, in the form of property boundaries, vernacular buildings, churches, public buildings and roads, means that sketch mapping on to an OS 25in map produces as accurate a plan as is normally required. Building surveys can be carried out on dated examples of buildings, and styles of architecture can also be recorded. Another valuable exercise is to mark on breaks of slope and change of level within the town or village. Such features can indicate lines of old roads, lost town defences, or precincts. In villages the recording of existing property boundaries with associated earthworks can add to any study of the earlier topography of the settlement. Similarly breaks of slopes can be used to demonstrate the development of the settlement. It may also be possible to compare the plans of the present village with those of the Middle Ages. Over a period of time regular fieldwork correlated with documentary work and any excavations, archaeological or non-archaeological, carried out within the village or town area can result in the acquisition of much new topographical information.

BUILDINGS

The recording of smaller vernacular buildings can be as valuable as the study of prominent buildings. Such work has been carried out on building materials, and this can often be relevant to topographical studies. Similarly the recording of periods of buildings within a settlement will be immensely valuable as a guide to periods of prosperity, fashion and construction techniques at the time of building. The method of recording used here is cartographic and, if a code can be established, the OS 25in or 50in maps provide a good basis for most plans. Brunskill's building record cards provide a good framework for recording building materials and styles within any one place or over a wide area (Appendix 3). It must, however, be remembered that this particular approach was largely designed with the study of older industrial housing in northern England in mind. If an extensive regional survey is planned, it might be advisable for the fieldworker or group to design their own local building card. Similarly this method relies exclusively on exterior evidence and it has been frequently shown that the interior structure might tell a very different story. The fieldworker who wishes to become proficient in the study of vernacular buildings as part of his topographical studies would do well to study the extensive literature, but a few rules of thumb can be noted.[15]

1. An outline plan of a building, particularly if additions and alterations are readily distinguishable, can be a useful starting point. The persistence of buildings with two or three main units (hall, parlour or private rooms, and service or kitchen end) up to the seventeenth century is now well established, and may help with the study of a building's growth or development.
2. Within the building plan the position of features such as chimneystacks, passages, doorways and kitchens may be of significance and should be noted. In early houses the main doorways are often at each end of a passage two-thirds of the way along the main wall; to one side of this is the service area, while the main body of the house consists of hall and parlour. The main stack is usually in the hall, and often against the passage.
3. The roof is the best place to look in any suspected old building, since original carpentry work may survive there when the rest of the building has been altered.
4. With some reservations, any dated features provide known fixed points in the study of a building, but it is as well to bear in mind the common re-use of materials and the replacement of buildings on the same site.

Plans can be produced easily with graph paper and tapes. The thickness of the wall should be marked out from window and door openings, and diagonals of rooms checked to record irregular room areas, since many old houses are far from rectangular. Elevations inside can be achieved by drawing a section (as in archaeological drawing) of each room or space on each floor, provided that the sections are linked by measurements between storeys. Again sketch plans or drawings may be the quickest way of recording.

PLACE-NAMES

Town, village, street and field names can all help enormously with understanding the landscape. The study of place-names is specialised and the English Place-Name Society is producing a complete survey county by county.[16] Many areas, however, have not yet been covered, and it is still possible to discover previously unidentified archaeological sites from minor place-names. Later in the book (p 115) we indicate ways in which place-name studies can help with landscape interpretation.

QUESTIONNAIRES

A valuable technique of standardising the approach to different types of earthwork site is provided by the questionnaire; that reproduced in Appendix 4 was designed by the Medieval Village Research Group. The Moated Sites Research Group have produced a different version, emphasising that the wide variety of questions asked can be used as a model for the examination of other types of site (Appendix 5)

PRODUCTION OF FINISHED PLANS AND MAPS

If plans made in the field are to be of value to anyone other than the fieldworker, and if they are to be published, they will need to be drawn up in a finished and presentable form. Plain white paper is adequate for many plans, but where a number of dye-line copies are required, the plan needs to be of better quality and must be drawn on transparent paper. Ordinary tracing paper shrinks and distorts over a period of time, and one of the plastic-based transparent films should be used to avoid this.

If the plan is to be published, the draughtsman should have an idea of the degree of reduction required. There are several books and papers to help fieldworkers producing plans.[17] It is often useful to pin the plan on the wall of a room and see how the features merge when viewed from a distance. The drawing can be done with a variety of instruments and with permanent Indian ink. Mapping pens are best for hachures, but other work is probably best done with the Graphos or Radiograph ranges of pens and nibs. Frequent use of these pens will make the operator competent to get the best out of them. Mistakes can be obliterated with the use of 'Snowpake' or 'Process White'. Lettering can be done either with stencils, of which there is a wide range on the market, or one of the brands of dry-transfer or self-adhesive lettering. These are sold under trade names such as 'Letraset' and 'Pressletta'. Plans for publication should be drawn on plastic-based planning films, which are dimensionally stable under all normal changes of temperature or humidity. These are sold under trade names such as 'Permatrace', 'Velvetex', 'Etherlon', and 'Ozalid'.

Notes and references to this chapter begin on p 184

CHAPTER 3

Maps and Landscape Archaeology

The landscape historian should realise from the beginning that for him the principal document is outside the library in the field and that, although he may well find clues and help from the written work of others, normally he will have to tread a lonely path and locate almost all his own evidence. The fieldworker is principally concerned with recording, and in the light of the rate of current change it is most important that this record is made. The synthesis of landscape evidence can often wait until afterwards. The fieldworker does, however, have a wide range of literary and documentary sources at his disposal to help direct or elucidate some aspects of his work. There is a long tradition of local historical studies in Great Britain and, like any student of British history, the fieldworker has a great corpus of written work behind him. Almost invariably this work will have been undertaken for purposes other than the reconstruction of past landscapes, but information and clues are none the less frequently available in published form. Before undertaking a fieldwork project, the student is therefore strongly advised to acquaint himself with the published sources relating to his area or topic. As well as individual parish or church histories, the most likely printed source will be contained within the proceedings or transactions of the relevant County Archaeological Society[1] or in the *Victoria County History* (Appendix 1).

It is not our function to discuss purely documentary evidence in any detail. It is an area that has been well covered by others, and there is much relevant literature on the location and interpretation of available archival material.[2] Nevertheless, if the project is to be covered in depth and published, the fieldworker must at least be aware of the documentary sources at his disposal. However, it must be emphasised that it is surprisingly difficult precisely to relate features on the ground to documentary references. The most frequently quoted instance is the record of a mill in the Domesday Survey which is often misleadingly identified with the site of an extant or recently abandoned mill. It is extremely unlikely that the eleventh-century mill would have occupied exactly the same site as the modern structure, for mills, like other vernacular buildings, were regularly destroyed and rebuilt throughout the Middle Ages. A long run of documents may help to locate the site more accurately, but considerable caution is required when making geographical assumptions of continuity based on documentary sources.

Nevertheless it is sometimes possible to pinpoint the site of a feature referred to in a document. For example, there is a reference to *fossatores* and other workmen digging trenches, excavating the moat and putting up a new barricade round the site of the new castle at Beaumaris.[3] Normally such references are to large royal structures, and yet hidden away in manorial rolls there may occasionally be a precise reference to the existence or construction of a small earthwork. The thirteenth-century *Red Book of Worcester*[4] tells of islands in fishponds at Alvechurch (Worcs) which can still be recognised on the ground today (Fig 11).[5] Late thirteenth- and early fourteenth-century documents mention a moat (literally 'dug out waters'), a fishery, two islands in that fishery, a mill pool and two mills. One mill survives and a house has been built on the site of the Bishop of Worcester's Palace, but the other features survive only in earthwork form. Similarly a park with a large fishpond is recorded from the twelfth century at Feckenham, Worcestershire (Fig 11), and a late fifteenth-century account of the rebuilding of a water mill at Midhurst (Sussex) includes a reference to diverting the water and ramming the retaining banks.[6] Nevertheless on the building of hundreds of small motte and bailey castles in the twelfth century and many other minor medieval earthworks the documents are almost completely silent.

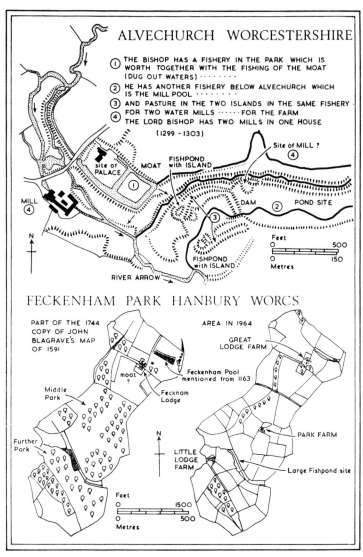

Fig 11 Alvechurch and Hanbury, Worcestershire. The palace of the Bishops of Worcester at Alvechurch was surrounded by a moat, a fishery and mills, all of which are mentioned in documents, 1299–1303. Feckenham Park in Hanbury belonged to the Crown and there are several surviving references to the park and fishponds

CARTOGRAPHIC EVIDENCE

By far the most important document to the fieldworker is the map, both as a source and a tool. Apart from the enormous national archives of maps and plans in the national repositories,[7] there are myriad smaller collections in libraries and archives throughout the country.[8] Because of the dramatic landscape changes of the past century, maps recording town and country before 1900 are of importance to the fieldworker. Despite their difference in purpose, physical form, detail and accuracy, they are the closest the fieldworker can get to an accurate representation of past landscapes. At its simplest, a map represents the cartographer's attempt to portray aspects of the countryside in plan form. Inevitably the production of a map involves a considerable element of choice on the part of the mapmaker, who will omit some features while overemphasising others according to the function of the finished product.

The value of any map is likely to be determined by its original function and the methods employed by the cartographer. Early maps were drawn up by tradesmen, craftsmen and artists as well as scientific surveyors. When dealing with such maps, the fieldworker should make some attempt to assess the techniques and accuracy of any cartographer on whom he is relying for evidence. A survey of early maps and plans has recently been published and should be consulted.[9] Some cartographers, like John Speed, were antiquarians interested in historical features. Isaac Taylor was a keen amateur archaeologist, and some of his county maps, including Dorset (1765), provide the fullest distribution of field antiquities before the Ordnance Survey. John Rocque, on the other hand, paid little attention to archaeological features, but emphasised his interest in land utilisation by the prominent depiction of parks, plantations and other aspects of land management.

The fieldworker will naturally find that large-scale maps provide the most information for his task. In some instances county maps do show pertinent information, and may present the only pictorial or documentary evidence of, for instance, a deer park or chapel. There is no national gazetteer of plans, and though some counties are well served with their own survey of maps, others have no such guide.[10] However, a useful general starting point is provided by R. A. Skelton's *County Atlases of the British Isles* (1970).

How can the fieldworker make the most effective use of old maps? A casual glance may be enough to indicate the main features of a village or area, but a more instructive technique is to transcribe the plan into a form comparable with modern OS plans. This can be done by photographing the plan and reproducing it at a size similar to the OS 6in or 25in maps, or by tracing off the original. It is then possible to take a tracing from a photograph, orientate it with the National Grid and compare the features on the old plan with those on the modern map. This procedure also gives one an opportunity of checking the accuracy of the original plan (Fig 15). Invariably there will be some constant features – a stream, a property boundary, the church or the manor house – and from the degree of difference an assessment of the plan's authenticity can be made. Fig 11, for example, shows the use of this technique to compare a sixteenth-century map of Feckenham Park (Worcs) with the modern ordnance survey map. If the original plan is shown to be inaccurate, an attempt can be made on the amended version to correct the errors. The fieldworker is advised to make the copy on good tracing paper or, preferably, tracing film, using black Indian ink. This plan can then be photocopied or reproduced by dye-line process. Equipped with several copies of the plan the fieldworker can then visit the area, and earthwork features or other relevant surviving elements of buildings or properties can be marked on the plans in coloured pencils.

An alternative method is to make a direct tracing off the original map and then use manual cartographic techniques, or some form of scale-changing instrument (a visualiser), to reduce or enlarge the map to the required scale. (Visualisers are generally known under the trade names of Grant projectors, Hubex visualisers, Copy Scanner and Plan variographs, Map-Graphs and Optiscopes.) A less accurate, but speedy, method is to place the drawing under an epidiascope and project on to a map of the required scale; the projector can then be moved backwards and forwards until common features coincide. A final method is simply to transfer by eye information from the original map on to a modern plan. Such techniques as the last two should not be employed if the plans are to be published, unless an explanation of the probable degree of error is clearly indicated.

Given a good series of maps, including seventeenth- or eighteenth-century estate maps, enclosure or town maps, the tithe map, and the first edition of the OS 6in map, it is possible to record in graphic form the landscape changes in any one locality over 200 or 300 years. As this corresponds to a period of great topographical change, with enclosure, industrialisation and urban expansion, it is possible to illustrate recent landscape development in an extremely effective way. Fig 12 illustrates the application of this technique for the parish of Milton under Wychwood (Oxon).[11] The enclosure map (1850) shows the pre-enclosure landscape with its composite named furlongs. 'Hoarstone furlong' may well refer to a lost prehistoric mega-

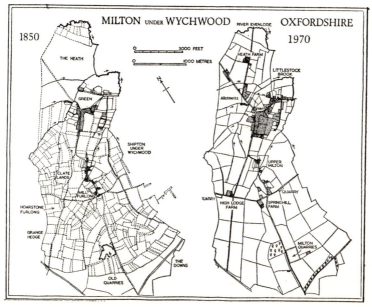

Fig 12 Milton under Wychwood, Oxfordshire, 1850 and 1970. The pattern of medieval topography was preserved until the enclosure of 1850. The 1970 layout shows the planned landscape of the nineteenth century and the expansion of the village in recent years

lithic monument, 'Clatelands' (claylands) is first recorded in the twelfth century and the mill on 'Mill Furlong' can be identified from earthworks in the valley bottom. Enclosure after 1850 resulted in the present landscape of tidy parish boundaries, straightened roads, regular field boundaries, new farms established outside the village and the provision of quarries and allotments. It shows too how the common heath has been enclosed into Heath Farm, and how the village green survived enclosure but only in a severely truncated form. This technique can also be valuable when applied to landscapes which have undergone less dramatic but none the less substantial changes. The Lanhydrock Atlas records a group of Cornish estates in the late seventeenth century which can be compared with the modern Ordnance Survey map (Fig 13). During this period a whole new settlement called Newbridge developed on the common moorland. It also includes the earliest known reference to the grist (corn) mill at Roskennal.

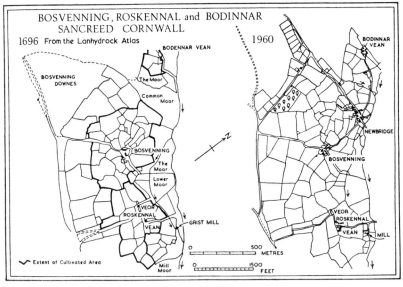

Fig 13 Bosvenning, Roskennal and Bodinnar, Sancreed, Cornwall. A comparison of the area in 1696 with a plan of 1960 shows that the field pattern has remained very similar in this area of early enclosure. One completely new settlement at Newbridge came into existence after 1696

Which features depicted on old maps are of particular value to the landscape historian? Very little can be dismissed as being totally irrelevant. The map represents a compendium of information, some of which may be available elsewhere, but to compile it in diagrammatic form would take many weeks of work. An aggregate list of the features to be found on old maps would amount to a complete inventory of the landscape, although naturally the fieldworker cannot expect to encounter all features on any one map. Town and village maps record the form of the settlements, with alignment of buildings and boundaries. The latter are of particular value in attempting to trace medieval tenement and property boundaries. Some maps carry valuable information about a change in the settlement pattern. Fig 14, for instance, portrays part of the village of Atcham (Shropshire)

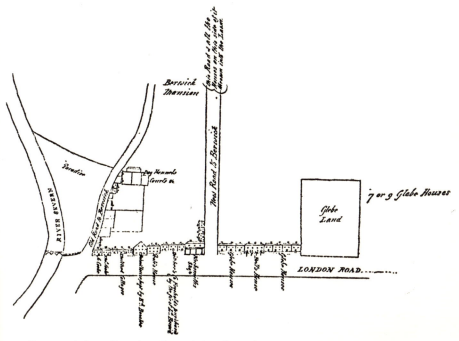

Fig 14   Atcham, Shropshire. Part of the village, which was destroyed by the extension of Attingham Park, taken from a late eighteenth-century map. Notice the prospects of various buildings

in the eighteenth century.[12] An area of the village which disappeared with the extension of Attingham Park is depicted, together with the surveyor's comment 'this Road & all the Houses on this side of it thrown into the Lawn'.

On some maps, particularly those compiled before 1700, the main buildings may have been drawn in elevation or perspective, sometimes providing an architectural record of church, manor house, court house, inn, almshouse, barn or school and even outbuildings. It is occasionally possible to distinguish roofing materials of tile or thatch, and discern which windows had glass. In some instances important structural information is recorded. The plate on p 18 shows a possible cruck gable-end of the manor house at Middleton Stoney (Oxon) in 1737.[13] This building was subsequently removed with the rest of the village when the park was extended in the early nineteenth century. Greens and market places on early maps are particularly valuable in reconstructing the early form of the settlement.

On pre-enclosure maps the complex of strips and closes in the village is precisely recorded. In hilly parishes lynchets may be distinguished or boundary stones may have been plotted. The maps also had a tenurial function recording ownership, tenancy and farm and field size. They provide an early record of land utilisation in some cases: arable, meadow and pasture, and occasionally crops and rotations are identified; wood, marsh, heath and moor may be depicted; and orchards, gardens, fishponds, dovecotes, mills and leats, vineyards, flax pieces and hopyards help to elucidate the village economy. Parkland was often recorded in detail – woodlands and glades, fenced lawns, ornamental gardens and grottoes; and the plans of landscape gardeners (projected and completed) also reveal intimate details of local change.[14] The creation of a small park from an ancient warren at Rousham (Oxon) is illustrated by the comparison of two maps of 1721 and 1955 (Fig 15). This design by William Kent, and the work of other landscape architects, resulted in a complete change of the village topography.

Sites of rural industries are commonly recorded on old maps. These can include furnaces and glass houses; brick, tile and lime kilns; and

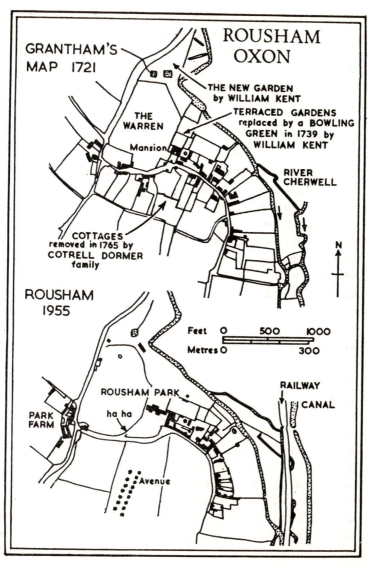

Fig 15   Rousham, Oxfordshire. A comparison between the maps of 1721 and 1955 shows that the village was greatly altered by the emparking activities of William Kent and others

pits for chalk, sand, gravel and marl. This last category is particularly important, as such features when overgrown can often be interpreted as being of archaeological importance. Tanning yards and saltings are also included, as well as a variety of mills – wind, water and tide, fulling, corn and paper.[15] The major and minor roads and streets, lanes and droveways, bridleways and tracks, toll-bars, fords, bridges (sometimes with structural information) and ferries are also surveyed.

Field names are particularly valuable and there are many instances where an archaeological site or earthwork has been identified from an estate map. For instance, the field names *Old Town, Townpiece* or *Townend*, can often mark the site of a deserted village.[16] The field name *Blacklands* may also identify the site of a former, but not necessarily medieval settlement, the 'black' referring to the dark soil caused by accumulated debris of former occupation. Other elements found in minor place-names which may help identify archaeological sites are *hlaw* (OE) and *haugr* (Sc), meaning barrow or tumulus; *cest* and *lic* (OE), indicating places where a coffin or a body was discovered at some time; *hord* (OE) referring to a place where treasure has been found, or more probably thought to have been buried; and *crocc* (OE), meaning crock or earthenware pot and perhaps pointing to the presence of a settlement or even a cemetery site.

In some instances maps record relict or archaeological features in considerable detail. A particularly striking example of this is the deserted village of Boarstall (Bucks), which is depicted on a plan of 1444 that must surely rank as the earliest English village plan.[17] A comparison of the map with the earthworks on the ground is particularly revealing, and demonstrates that, although impressionistic, the fifteenth-century cartographer was reasonably accurate, and even included the ridge and furrow around the village (Fig 16). Only the tower gatehouse and church are constant buildings on the two maps, and the latter has lost its own tower. In other instances settlements had been deserted and the earthworks were recorded as being the site of an old township. A case in point is the recently discovered plan of East Layton (Co Durham), where the cartographer wrote 'the scyte of the houses' over empty crofts adjoining the village green.

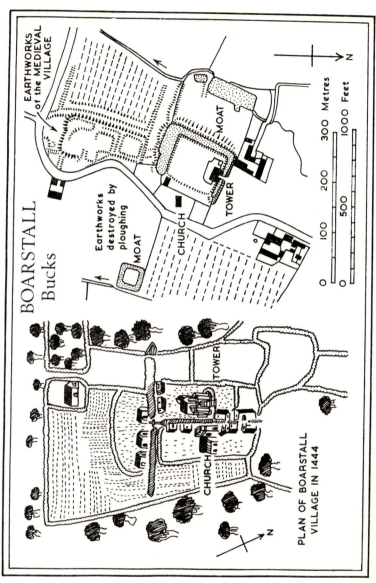

Fig 16 Boarstall, Buckinghamshire. Plan of 1444 compared with a sketch map of the earthworks in 1972. The earlier plan shows a prospect of the village before it was deserted. The tower and church are common to both maps, which are not to the same scale

Similarly on a late sixteenth-century plan of Fallowfield (Northumberland) the draughtsman recorded the deserted portion of the village with eight small dotted rectangles.[18]

The fieldworker undertaking the study of a small region consisting of, say, half a dozen parishes should try to produce a plan of the parish boundaries as they were before the middle of the nineteenth century. The first editions of the OS and Tithe maps are particularly valuable, as the maps were generally drawn up before the boundaries were changed. After this date there was considerable parochial reorganisation, resulting in the amalgamation of some parishes and the rationalisation of many parish boundaries. These alterations changed a boundary pattern which in many areas dated back at least to the Middle Ages, often giving clues as to ancient manorial and estate boundaries. Fig 17 shows an example of this in the parish of Halesowen (Worcs), which until the nineteenth century contained the vestiges of medieval estates from both the counties of Worcester-

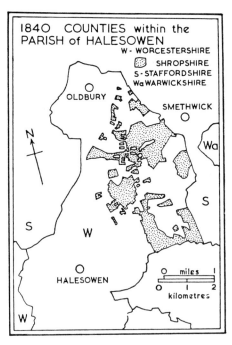

Fig 17 Halesowen, Worcestershire. Counties within the parish in 1840. This pattern is the result of a twelfth-century division of the manor. Based on first edition OS 1in maps

shire and Shropshire inextricably mixed in strip form. Similarly, when studying a town, a plan of property boundaries based on the earliest large-scale map should be drawn, so that the fieldworker can check whether they have survived, by using both later plans and the field evidence.

Some of the most effective fieldwork can be based upon composite plans, of the type included in recent volumes of the *Victoria County History* for the counties of Wiltshire and Oxfordshire. These use the tithe maps as a basis, but add information from earlier large-scale estate maps, to provide a reasonably comprehensive plan.

TOWN MAPS AND PLANS

Maps and plans of towns are obviously an important source of information, providing evidence on the development and form of rapid topographical change. However, the availability of town maps varies considerably. Many of our provincial towns have a series of plans dating from the sixteenth century, while other smaller centres surprisingly enough have no cartographic record until the nineteenth century. Sometimes nothing exists before the large-scale post-1854 OS plans, and some are as late as 1893. The development of urban cartography is well described in J. B. Harley's *Maps for the Local Historian* (1972), but reference should be made to the work of John Speed, who in the *Theatre of the Empire of Great Britain* (1612) portrayed seventy-three towns. These maps are relatively accurate, but the fieldworker should be wary of taking them at their face value. Speed's plans create additional problems in that they were often copied and republished, with the errors compounded, during the following 150 years, and this is a danger common to many early maps; but, bearing in mind the function for which many of them were made (some for housing, some for transport), and the associated omissions and errors, such plans can be of the greatest help to the urban fieldworker.

ESTATE MAPS

It has been estimated that there are over 20,000 private estate maps in archives, libraries and collections throughout the country.[19] The great majority show only small estates or a single farm, but some cover whole or several parishes. They are not easy to find, however. Printed catalogues of maps continue to appear slowly; they normally include enclosure and tithe award maps, public schemes (canals, railways, turnpike roads etc) and other official maps, as well as private estate maps. They exist for Bedfordshire (1930), Essex (1947), West Sussex (1962), Berkshire (1954) and Lancashire (1950) (enclosure maps only); most local record offices' *Guides* list them briefly. The National Repositories in London, Oxford and Cambridge have large numbers relating to private estates, and photocopies or photographs of plans can usually be obtained.

ENCLOSURE AND TITHE MAPS

While estate plans resulted from the local management of private property, enclosure and tithe maps were the result of legislative activity of a far-reaching nature, resulting from either private enclosures connected with the General Enclosure Acts of 1836 and 1845 or the Tithe Commutation Act of 1836. Enclosure and tithe maps tend to complement each other. While parliamentary enclosure surveys are mainly spread out over the century or so after 1750, the tithe maps are concentrated in the middle decades of the nineteenth century. Additionally those areas richest in enclosure, such as Northamptonshire, tend to be correspondingly weak in tithe maps, since at the time of enclosure the tithes were usually commuted, removing the need for a full survey by the Tithe Commissioners. Conversely, counties in the south-east and south-west, with few parliamentary enclosure acts, were almost completely covered by tithe awards.

The enclosure movements which culminated in the Georgian era had antecedents dating back to the Middle Ages, but in many areas it was the activities of the Parliamentary Commission that dramatically reshaped the countryside. In many parts of central England the Enclosure Commissioners virtually planned a new landscape of regular fields, roads and drains (Fig 12). Occasionally the boundaries of the former commons and open fields are depicted on the surveyors' maps. It is certainly normal for their maps to distinguish clearly the old enclosures, while some give the positions of village houses and buildings. The acts related to something like 5,000 ancient parishes in England and several hundred in Wales. A basic distinction should be drawn between two major groups of enclosures – firstly, those relating to the common arable fields and common meadows, and, secondly, those relating to the other commons, such as heath, marsh and moorland, generally known as waste. The most readily available lists of English enclosure awards are the county handlists prepared by W. E. Tate, usually published in the county archaeological society *Proceedings* or *Transactions*, but these are not complete.[20]

The tithe surveys extended to some 11,800 parishes or townships in England and Wales, covering just under 80 per cent of the area.[21] The maps furnished the first large-scale survey of much of the country, predating the OS 6in and 25in maps by almost a generation. The surveys' two principal documents are the plans and the written apportionments, which were designed to be used together. The end result is an almost exhaustive local inventory, including details of settlement, parish, field and farm boundaries; land use; field names; the extent of common, heaths and greens; the progress of enclosure; and the intricacies of tenure. Not least, in many industrial areas, tithe maps record conditions towards the end of the early railway age. The tithe documents were prepared in triplicate. One copy remained in the custody of the Tithe Redemption Commission, and was transferred to the Public Record Office.[22] A second copy was deposited with the Diocesan Records, and the third with the incumbent of the parish. The first copies survive complete, providing a central national archive, but the survival of the other two is more patchy, although County Record Offices have normally managed to obtain quite a good coverage. An almost complete set of tithe maps for Wales is in the National Library of Wales. The tithe survey did not extend to Scotland.

ORDNANCE SURVEY MAPS

The Ordnance Survey, or Trigonometrical Survey as it was originally named, was founded in 1791 with the primary object of preparing a map of Great Britain on a scale of 1in to 1 mile. The first OS 1in map of Kent was privately published in 1801, and the first numbered sheets of the official series of 1in maps appeared in 1805. Since then the Ordnance Survey has produced tens of thousands of plans on different scales. A full guide to these plans for fieldworkers has been produced in J. B. Harley and C. W. Phillips's *The Historian's Guide to Ordnance Survey Maps* (1964).[23] Here it is only necessary to point to those maps the fieldworker will find most useful.

Even now it is unlikely that the full potential of the OS large-scale maps has been realised as a source of local history. The early plans in themselves represent historical documents of major importance. To field archaeologists the maps provide indispensable clues to the material remains of the past, and the fieldworker will find the OS 1in maps, both past and present, of the greatest value when acquainting himself with a region or studying a general theme, such as changes in parkland or the development of settlement.[24] The 1in sheet, incidentally, provides a shorthand guide to archaeological fieldwork already carried out in, for instance, the use of different typefaces to indicate the supposed date of sites and finds, but the fieldworker is more likely to find detailed evidence on the larger 6in and 25in scale plans. These plans will probably coincide in scale with those used in the field and are therefore considerably easier to correlate.

The OS 25in maps delineate the landscape with great detail and accuracy. In fact practically all the significant man-made features to be found on the ground are depicted. The first record of many features is on the earliest edition, and as a topographical record the series transcends all previous maps. Every road, field, fence or hedge, stream and building are shown; non-agricultural land is distinguished as woodland, marsh and rough pasture; quarries and sand, gravel and clay pits are depicted separately; all administrative boundaries, civil and ecclesiastical, are shown; and prehistoric, Roman and medieval antiquities are marked, as well as hundreds of minor place-names. The exact shape and area of each enclosure is maintained, the series being the first to show field boundaries with complete accuracy. Many watermills are named, and the uses of industrial premises given. On occasions the remaining strips and other vestiges of open fields and common meadows may be recorded. Sometimes the surveyors even record the earthworks of moated and deserted village sites without realising their significance, and these plans contain the most comprehensive survey of castle earthworks ever undertaken in this country.

During the nineteenth century a series of large-scale plans was issued, starting in 1840 with 1: 1056 scale maps for towns with a population of 4,000 or more to the north of the Preston–Hull line, and following up with a series of town plans 1: 1056 or 5ft to 1 mile (1843–94) and another at 1: 528 or 10ft to 1 mile (1855–95). Such maps are invaluable today because they take us one step nearer lost landscapes of the post-medieval period and contain clues relating to even earlier landscapes.

It is worth recording, at this point, the criteria on which the Ordnance Survey bases its archaeological data. All recognised extant archaeological earthworks are surveyed by the Archaeology Division. The details of all other earthworks, natural and artificial, are the responsibility of surveyors without archaeological experience, who are required to show only those features which exceed a survey criterion of 1m in height. Archaeology Division surveyors may show any archaeological feature less than 1m in height if the feature is such that a layman may recognise it readily with the map as a guide. This is not to say that all ancient slope detail is supplied, as in practice this would overbalance the Ordnance Survey map. Generally speaking, the Division excludes all the following features unless a competent authority can be found to state that they are of outstanding importance: all post-Norman buildings and their subsidiary features, field systems, minor quarrying (unless associated with a building of more than local interest, such as an abbey), bridges, fishponds, mill leats and catchment pools. Some exceptions are made, as with deserted villages, where field and house plots are usually surveyed and recorded on the larger-scale plans.

Archaeological and historical maps
The Ordnance Survey publishes a series of archaeological maps with texts, including *Roman Britain* (scale 1: 1,000,000), *Britain in the Dark Ages* (scale 1: 1,000,000) and *Monastic Britain* (scale 1: 625,000).

These sheets provide a useful introduction to the geographical distribution of antiquities, although inevitably some are incomplete, owing to the large increase in the number of known sites and finds over the past few years.

The National Grid

All modern Ordnance Survey maps carry the National Grid, a series of squares with sides respectively parallel and at right-angles to the straight line that represents the central meridian of Ordnance Survey mapping. The sides of the grid squares are multiples of 1m, and with their assistance every point in Great Britain acquires a unique map reference. The national grid reference of a point remains the same whatever the scale of the map in use, but the precision to which it can be given depends on the scale. Thus reference can be given by eye to an accuracy of 10m on the 1:1250 and 1:2500 scale maps, to 100m on 1in maps, and to 1km on ¼in maps. The Ordnance Survey produces a *Gazetteer of Great Britain* (revised 1972) which gives the national grid references of all places named on their ¼in maps.

Copyright

Fieldworkers should be aware that if a map is drawn or reproduced from an OS plan less than 50 years old, it needs copyright clearance. In case of doubt consult the Publications Department of the Survey.

Notes and references to this chapter begin on p 185

CHAPTER 4

Aerial Photography

With the refinement of aerial photographic techniques, air photographs have become an increasingly important aid to field archaeology.[1] Serious archaeological recording began after World War I when O. G. S. Crawford, the first Archaeology Officer of the Ordnance Survey, produced a number of pioneer books on the subject.[2] Initially much of this work concentrated on prehistoric earthwork sites, and it was not until the 1930s that the photography of cropmarks was developed and refined.[3] Since then there has been an increasing use of, and reliance on, air photographs by geographers and historians, as well as archaeologists. However, it is probably true to say that the full and most effective use of aerial photography still remains to be developed in landscape studies.

If the fieldworker is fortunate enough to have access to a passenger seat on a light aeroplane, a few trips at the right time of day and year might be sufficient to provide a considerable amount of information about the distribution and nature of medieval earthworks within a given area. It would undoubtedly be valuable for more fieldworkers to take photographs, but the unsystematic collection of more aerial photographic data without a general policy for recording is unsatisfactory. There are, too, problems which result from the large number of existing photographs; these require storage, recording, and, most important of all, analysis. There is a good case for the aerial photography of archaeological sites to be organised on the lines of a research project, with certain areas being intensively examined over a number of years. Such an examination could be invaluable in the case of cropmarks, which vary substantially in quality from year to year. Nevertheless new aerial photography and the consultation of existing air coverage should be an intrinsic part of any research or rescue operation, whether it is concerned with a single archaeological site or larger tracts of land.

Aerial photographs can be used as a way of examining well known sites or areas, including cropmark complexes and earthworks. The air photograph comprehends in a glance, and records permanently, a broad sweep of countryside. The aerial camera records small irregularities on the ground and makes them lucid as they are seen from a distance. Their relation to other features, often invisible on the ground, becomes apparent. It is true that more prominent physical remains of the Middle Ages can be recorded on a map, but in this case each feature is conventionalised and the reader must interpret the symbols and make his own mental image. Nor can a map convey the true texture of the landscape; an air photograph makes no selection and employs no convention. On a map the fence, hedge or stone wall will all be recorded by the same convention, and ephemeral details such as crops and vegetation are omitted. A photograph will record not only such major features as are commonly delineated on a map, but a wealth of minor and often impermanent details never found on the largest general survey. Accordingly aerial photographs can be used for the examination of previously unrecorded areas and the recording of large areas of minor earthworks. They can also be extremely valuable for the study of village and town plans, and general settlement patterns. Even with large-scale or highly detailed plans a great deal can still be learnt from air photographs of any particular place, since the viewpoint provided is still largely unfamiliar to most people. Views can either be vertical, where the camera points straight down, or oblique, where the view is recorded at an angle.

EARTHWORKS

There are still hundreds of square miles of medieval features on the ground surface of Britain, the earliest landscape surviving over large areas still remaining to be recorded. The earthworks of earlier landscapes of the Iron Age or the Romano-British period survive only in pockets, but traces of medieval settlement, defence and agriculture survive in earthwork form over considerable areas of rural Britain. Earthworks are of fundamental importance to medieval studies, and aerial photographs of these can be of the greatest assistance in their recording and interpretation. Photographs of earthworks are best taken when highlights and shadowed areas are evident, for then features are picked out in the manner illustrated in diagram A in Fig 18 (see also plates on pp 154, 171). Low-angled sunlight with the light at 90 degrees to slopes is ideal. Such conditions often obtain in the early morning and late evening in the autumn, winter and spring, but at some places, because of the inclination and aspect of an area, low light may not be of much help. Earthworks on a south-facing slope may be particularly difficult to photograph. Some earthworks can be extremely elusive: at Hen Domen (Montgomeryshire), for instance, an attempt to photograph the pre-Conquest ridge and furrow involved the use of car headlights at night.[4] The effect was to highlight the ridges and hollows more effectively than low sunlight. Drifts of leaves, hoar frost and snow into hollows or up against banks, and the differential melting of snow in hollows sheltered from the sun, can also reveal hitherto unrecognised features.

Vertical views of earthworks are particularly good for plotting areas of medieval ridge and furrow, parklands or settlement plans.[5] Many of the photographs taken by the RAF and commercial firms, incidentally, record such features, although they are frequently taken from too high an altitude to give the clarity required for the illustration of smaller earthworks. Overlapping vertical air photographs are particularly valuable; they should be examined through a stereoscopic viewer, which throws the ground features into three-dimensional relief. Alternatively oblique air photographs taken in low light often provide spectacular views of monastic, castle and village sites, and may reveal previously unidentified outlying earthworks (see plates, pp 154, 171, 172).

Air photographs of earthwork sites require the careful consideration normally afforded to cropmark sites. However, unlike crop-

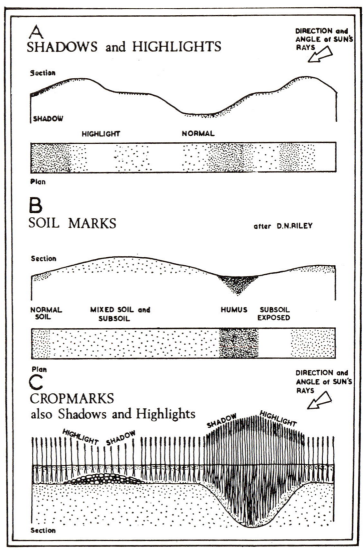

Fig 18 Diagrams of shadows and highlights, soil marks and cropmarks

marks, earthworks are visible on the surface, and the features on the air picture can therefore be checked with the field evidence. Because of the nature of this evidence, familiarity with the feature on the ground as a landscape element is obviously an important factor in understanding and interpreting air photographs. Nevertheless there are occasions when the landscape can only be understood when good aerial photographic cover becomes available. A major problem which commonly arises with earthworks, particularly those sites with steep-sided ditches, is the presence of a dense cover of trees and bushes which may obscure the underlying features, especially during the summer months.

It is also as well to remember that the earthworks revealed by aerial photography will frequently conceal layers of older structures, frequently rebuilt and not always on the same alignment. In the case of deserted villages this may mean that the house plans identified from the air are no older than the generation before the desertion of the site, and that within any site different areas may have been abandoned at different times.

TOWNSCAPES

Urban air photographs have tended to be under-used as a source for archaeological studies. Even given the existence of large-scale OS 25in and 50in maps of town centres, air pictures can still help illustrate many facets of urban topography. Vertical views provide valuable plans and often, because of shadows and building or roof lines, features of importance are emphasised more on an air photograph than on the equivalent map. Oblique photographs can place a town in its local context rather better than most maps, since the surrounding relief is often more obvious and the town's siting and arrangement can take on a new significance. For instance the plate on p 35 shows a vertical air view of Totnes (Devon) taken in intense sunlight from the south. The castle, the small walled enclosures of the Saxon *burh*, the burgage tenements of the medieval town and the small medieval suburb of Bridgtown Pomeroy across the river are clearly identifiable as separate elements.

Aerial Photography

CROPMARKS

Cropmarks are particularly important in prehistoric and Romano-British studies, but they can also be vital to the understanding of post-Roman landscapes and must therefore be considered here. Cropmarks are features normally only visible from the air, in the form of differential markings in fields carrying a cereal crop. Generally these marks represent either areas where the crop is riper and thus more bleached then the rest of the crop, or where it is less ripe and therefore much greener. Such marks are normally a function of the subsoil, principally of its depth and richness and the amount of available moisture. Darker lines may indicate the presence of filled ditches, where deep root penetration leads to slow-ripening plants; and lighter lines will reflect wall foundations or roads, where resistance to growth results in less luxuriant plants which will ripen earlier than the main crop (diagram C, Fig 18). Deep-rooting plants tend to give a clearer picture than shallow-rooting. Although grain crops, particularly barley, give the best cropmarks, clover and sugar beet provide rough indications, and differential growth can even be distinguished in pea and bean fields. Archaeological markings in grass are generally only present early in the year, except in severe drought, when dried-out areas or parch-marks may appear. Cropmarks result from ditched or buried features whose earthworks have been ploughed out, and as such they represent an erased landscape which nevertheless may have existed in earthwork form not long ago. It is, therefore, just as important to record and understand these features, which often bear little relation to the modern landscape, as it is to record surviving earthworks.

Recent work using the same groups of sites each year over a period of years has suggested that there are 10–14 days per year in mid to late July when the marks are best seen as the crops are ripening. In good years, such as 1959 and 1970, as long a period as 3 weeks may be available, while some marks may be visible throughout the growing period. It is, however, more economical to collect the information during the optimum period. About one year in seven is particularly good for cropmarks.

Types of crop may also have an effect on the vividness of the cropmarks produced. New strains of cereal send out their roots horizontally, so that the development of deep roots to the water level, which is such an important factor in cropmark formation, may not take place. Alternatively, a period of drought coinciding with germination and early crop development can encourage roots to go down vertically and cropmarks may be apparent throughout the crop's growth. If crops are planted close together, a separate humidity may be created under the plants, which may even draw up surface soil water, thus destroying the cropmark effect over a ditch. As they ripen, the heads of barley grain drop over to one side; so in order to record different colours in the crop it is usually necessary for the photographer to circle in a series of loops over the area in which he is interested.

The character of the subsoil is of great importance; generally the more porous it is the better the chance of cropmarks. Valley or plateau gravel, and Jurassic and Carboniferous limestone produce good cropmarks, but sand and sandstone are of little use. Sites on clay do not manifest themselves at all well, and even on valley gravels patches of clay are to be found effectively masking traces of earlier occupation. All these factors may affect the nature and value of cropmark features.

Only some of the buried features in the ground will manifest themselves as cropmarks. Often the most important part of the site can be revealed only by excavation, which involves complete removal of the topsoil. For this reason any group of cropmarks can be taken only as an indication of part of what is buried – in fact, as a clue to the hidden evidence. The beginner should be aware of a number of deceptive markings such as the 'envelope pattern', which results from concentric ploughing techniques and harvesting but appears in photographs in the form of a regular cropmark, and circular patterns, which may result from a range of agricultural activities. In some areas local drift geological conditions have given rise to natural cropmarks known as frost cracks. These can often be confused with man-made features, as can be seen in the plate on p 36, where traces of medieval settlement overlie an area of periglacial markings.[6]

Since it is often difficult to interpret the shape or arrangement of cropmarks, any description of a site should normally be based on the dimensions of features. It is often better to speak of 'ring ditches' and 'rectangular enclosures' than 'Bronze Age barrows' and 'Romano-British farmsteads', though detailed knowledge of a region may lead to an understanding of the types and forms of site likely to be encountered. Occasionally it may be possible to discern a relative chronology of features showing as cropmarks. For instance, it is sometimes possible to identify later medieval buildings built on top of earlier levelled ridge and furrow. In normal circumstances, however, archaeological excavation will be required to determine the relations between overlapping cropmarks. It should thus be made clear, in any cropmark publication, how much represents an objective description of the site and how much is the writer's subjective interpretation. In recent years there have been a number of cropmark surveys which have included impressive attempts at interpretation without excavation.[7] In the present state of British archaeology it is highly unlikely that every site can or should be excavated; such surveys are, therefore, of the greatest importance, in order to make accurate assessments about archaeological priorities.

As has already been indicated, there are few forms of cropmark exclusively attributable to the post-Roman period. The ploughed-out remains of Anglo-Saxon burial mounds from the air are virtually indistinguishable from Bronze Age round barrows. With practice the fieldworker may be able to distinguish the oval and rectangular dark patches characteristic of early Saxon sunken huts known as *grübenhauser*. In some instances early Saxon cemeteries can be identified, but these may appear identical with Romano-British burial sites. Recently some large rectangular structures have been identified and convincingly interpreted as Saxon palaces or halls; one such group was excavated at Yeavering (Northumberland).[8] As our understanding of the nature of early and mid Anglo-Saxon settlement develops, we may be able to recognise more readily the resulting cropmark features.[9] While it is true that most of the Anglo-Saxon sites identified and excavated to date have lain on porous soils and, theoretically at least, should show up as cropmarks, many of the buildings have proved to be so slight that, unless they are photographed under exceptional circumstances, they elude the camera.[10] Ploughed-out deserted medieval settlement sites are sometimes encountered as cropmarks, but ploughed-out ridge and furrow is more common (see plate, p 36), and is to be found on gravel terraces throughout southern and central Britain. There are other post-Roman features which may provide valuable evidence, notably ploughed-out linear boundaries, roads and park-banks.

Soil marks (Fig 18) appear after an earthwork site has been ploughed for the first time, but over the years the marks normally become blurred and disappear as the material from the earthwork is scattered over the field (see plate, p 153). In some conditions, notably with sites lying on chalk, the soil marks remain fresh for a considerable time. Soil marks show up wherever the fill of a ditch is a different colour from that of the surrounding soil, but buildings, banks and ridges will gradually merge with the rest of the field. Deep ploughing will hasten the process. During long dry spells in areas where there has been constant ploughing and the soil marks have nearly been ploughed out, buried features are sometimes revealed by dark or 'damp marks'.[11]

PLOTTING CROPMARKS AND EARTHWORKS ON TO MAPS

The most useful practical application of aerial photographs involves plotting cropmarks and earthwork features on to OS 6in or 25in maps. Only on these scales will the field boundaries, buildings and tracks likely to be present on air pictures show up in enough detail to provide a framework within which the features on the photograph can be plotted. Fig 19 shows a dense cropmark concentration plotted from oblique photographs on to an OS 6in plan of an area of Thames gravels near Abingdon (Oxon). This application of aerial photographs is particularly valuable in areas where mineral extraction is rapidly destroying large areas of archaeological material.

With vertical air photographs there are few problems in transferring the information to a map, providing that the photographs are correctly orientated with the plans, since normally only differences in scale have to be remedied. The features can be plotted on to the map by eye or by the use of proportional dividers or pieces of graph and tracing paper. If the plotter has access to a visualiser, this provides an alternative method, although some distortion may be encountered around the edges of the plan.

The situation is more difficult with oblique air photographs. If there is only one view, there is likely to be considerable distortion when features are drawn on to the map. However, provided there are a number of photographs taken from different angles or different heights, the problem becomes simpler, and the archaeological material can be readily aligned with features such as field boundaries already on the OS 6in map. The results can then be assessed by drawing oblique lines to join field boundaries and checking if the site or sites are sitting in the right part of the field. With oblique photographs there will always be some distortion in the shape of features, but this can be remedied by drawing their probable shape according to a subjective assessment. Quite apart from cropmarks, this method of plotting will be adequate for the production of rough outline plans of, say, a castle site or even the distribution of ridge and furrow.

SOURCES OF AERIAL PHOTOGRAPHS

Air photographs are taken for a great variety of purpose. Planners, developers, mapmakers, geologists, botanists and others all use aerial coverage today. However, many of these pictures do show archaeological sites and provide information about earlier landscapes which is not available elsewhere. It is thus important for fieldworkers in any particular area to be aware of all the potential sources of air photographs.

The National Monuments Record
An attempt is now being made by the Air Photographs Unit of the National Monuments Record (this is part of the RCAHM) to gather large numbers of air photographs together.[12] Most of the collection has been taken for archaeological purposes. The Unit also has photographs taken specifically for Royal Commission projects and for particular rescue schemes, such as the area to be covered by Peter-

Page 85 *Cricklade, Wiltshire.* Vertical air view of the centre of the Saxon burh. *The surviving street plan is probably Saxon and the existing properties, which may have originated as medieval burgages, now occupy only part of the defended area. The ridge and furrow on the right-hand side respects the line of Saxon defences*

Page 86 *Ludlow, Shropshire. Oblique air view of the town from the west. The line of the medieval town wall clearly demarcates an area of regular planned streets and properties. The original market area running from the church to the castle has been largely infilled; the southern extension of the castle bailey has obscured part of the original town plan and made a former road redundant (leaving a vacant area still evident today)*

borough New Town.[13] The collection may be visited by appointment, and there is limited working space for students. The pictures are indexed on a four-figure national grid reference system which can be easily read from the OS 1in map.

Ordnance Survey Archaeology Division[14]
The Division keeps a collection of principally non-archaeological air photographs which were selected because they show archaeological sites. These include old RAF pictures, more recent pictures taken as part of the Ordnance Survey's map revision work, and also a considerable number of original photographs collected by O. G. S. Crawford. A copy of much of this material has been deposited with the National Monuments Record in London. The collection is not normally accessible without prior arrangement with the Division. The OS regional offices have collections of vertical air photographs at 25in to 1 mile taken for map revision purposes, and these can normally be seen by arrangement.

Cambridge Committee for Aerial Photography[15]
Part of Cambridge University, the Committee has the largest collection of aerial photographs in Britain. Many of the photographs were taken for archaeological purposes and, apart from large numbers of cropmark sites from all over Britain, the collection includes Prof St Joseph's many fine air pictures of low light earthwork sites. The pictures, which are numbered, are also cross-referenced by parish and six-figure grid systems. Most of the photographs are obliques, but there are also a considerable number of verticals. The collection is not normally accessible, but the Committee will supply prints. When asking for prints, the enquirer should include the names of the parishes concerned with the grid references.

Museums
Many provincial and county museums have begun to assemble local or regional air photograph collections for their own areas, basing them on the above sources and on their own efforts. One such is the Oxford City and County Museum. The Ashmolean Museum,

Fig 19 Drayton, Berkshire. Map of multi-period cropmarks on the terrace gravels of the River Thames

Aerial Photography

Oxford, houses the original air photographs taken by Major Allen and Flt-Lt Riley in the 1930s and 1940s in Berkshire and Oxfordshire, some of which cover large areas of the Upper Thames Valley before large-scale gravel extraction began. Copies of the pictures can be ordered from the museum.

Non-archaeological sources
There are several commercial firms that take aerial photographs and carry out air surveys, among them BKS Surveys, Fairey Surveys, Meridian Airmaps, Aerofilms Ltd and Hunting Survey.[16] Although much of their material is not automatically available to fieldworkers, their collections, which may be seen on request, do contain many important archaeological and topographical photographs.

Development corporations, planning departments and other statutory bodies such as electricity, gas and water boards frequently have air surveys carried out for specific purposes, and again these can often be consulted. The amount of new or additional information likely to be contained therein varies with the conditions and time of year the survey was carried out. However, many do show cropmarks and others taken in low light give good earthwork coverage. Usually such photographs are verticals, taken for map or planning work and revision, and they are particularly useful, therefore, for a wide coverage of fields and villages. They are often taken at too small a scale for individual features to be well defined, since anything much smaller than 1: 15,000 is not very helpful except in the hands of specialists, but for wide landscape surveys they can be excellent.

Notes and references to this chapter begin on p 187

CHAPTER 5

Fieldwork in Towns

Over the past decade increasing interest has been paid to the shape and history of British towns.[1] The destruction of our ancient town centres is proceeding at such a rate, however, that there is still a real need for many more detailed urban topographical studies. In a recently published survey of British cities and towns it was estimated that one-fifth of the archaeological content of our historic towns will have been entirely destroyed by 1982 and another two-fifths will have been covered over by redevelopment.[2] A similar if not larger percentage of the above-ground buildings and topography is also threatened. As long ago as 1964 the Council for British Archaeology responded to the Buchanan Report on *Traffic in Towns*[3] by claiming that it clearly presented 'a choice between accessibility of all parts of a town to motor vehicles and the establishment of environmental areas'.[4] The Report itself spoke of historic town centres representing 'a major part of the heritage of the English-speaking world'. Until recently, however, there has been little practical response. A number of studies on the implications of urban redevelopment on archaeological material have been published,[5] but much urban planning still appears to neglect the historical townscape by destroying areas of early street plan and creating new structures which are often out of scale or sympathy with their more ancient neighbours. There has also been a tendency to concentrate on the preservation of single buildings rather than blocks or streets of buildings. This is the equivalent of keeping one piece from a chess set, even if it is the king, and replacing the rest of the pieces with draughtsmen.

Fieldwork in Towns

In this chapter we are concerned with towns founded or developed in the Anglo-Saxon and medieval periods. Many elements of these towns are still preserved in the plans of our modern cities, in the street pattern, and in the alignment of both ancient defences, properties and buildings.

Large towns often have extensive documentary archives, sometimes in published form, whereas small towns tend to possess fewer surviving documents; in these cases the topographical record is of particular value, as it may contain the only surviving information. The fieldworker can examine the layout of streets and lanes and the shape and size of building plots. He can also study the buildings, some of which will be of obvious architectural merit, while others are hidden behind later façades. The diligent worker should be able to dissect an urban landscape in the same way that a skilled archaeologist unravels the complicated story of a site through the analysis of plans and sections. He should be able to learn something about the original form and subsequent development of the centre he is studying, and to hazard intelligent guesses at the periods of prosperity, stagnation, and decline, and their causes.

It is often possible to identify a scale of survival of historical features within a town. This scale may enable the fieldworker to assess the relative importance of various features, and help with the understanding of a town's topography and the ages of certain areas and buildings. Frontages are changed most frequently, but behind many comparatively recent façades much older features often survive (see plate, p 103).

The requirements for a town's success include a geographical potential, a legal title and a social force. The geographical potential concerns the site chosen for the town and the nature and extent of the town's hinterland. The size and prosperity of any particular town will depend upon the capacity of the surrounding region to support an urban population that is not in the main agriculturally productive. A town can only exist in a commercial market-orientated economy, supported by a rural population which provides it with surplus produce. It was likely, therefore, that considerable effort had to be made in starting and nurturing a new town, and it was during these stages that a legal title, normally in the form of a borough charter, was particularly important, for it enabled merchants to obtain concessions on rents as well as raise money for the town by tolls.

THE SITE

The reasons for the siting and development of medieval towns are rarely well documented.[6] Although the actual location of a town is of prime importance in considering its origins, the fieldworker cannot assume that the centre of an earlier phase of development will coincide with the modern commercial centre.[7] Often the area of the old town has been completely surrounded by more recent urban development, and the modern centre may not correspond with that of the original town. Alternatively, industrial conurbations may have developed in a piecemeal manner from a series of villages, and here the fieldworker can try to reconstruct the pre-industrial landscape of village, field and common.

In some parts of the world there were spectacular examples of town sites being moved at different periods, with the result that deserted ancient sites now lie beside the modern town, but in Britain these movements only occurred with some Roman towns. For example, the Roman town of Wroxeter (*Viroconium*) lies adjacent to Shrewsbury, Shropshire, and the Roman town of Alchester lies 2 miles south-east of Bicester, Oxon. There are, however, a number of failed planted towns, particularly on the Welsh Marches, but few if any of these have later towns next to them[8] (Fig 22). Many towns were established next to existing villages whose form may have survived until the present day and be clearly distinguishable in the townscape. Some large conurbations have expanded to incorporate dozens of ancient settlements; traces of these too can be seen in parochial and street patterns, buildings and place-names.

What can be deduced from the place chosen to build a town or village? Local geography would have been a major factor, and the fieldworker should pay particular attention to streams, valleys, high land, areas of probable former marsh, well drained areas and level ground. Much of this information is available on the modern OS 2½in and 6in maps in the form of contour lines and spot heights.

Fieldwork in Towns

Particular attention should be paid to old watercourses and former marshy areas, even if they have long since disappeared, as they will have influenced the people considering the initial settlement. Some ancient watercourses have been channelled or piped so that the original appearance of the site may not be immediately apparent. One example is the Pool at Liverpool (Fig 20).

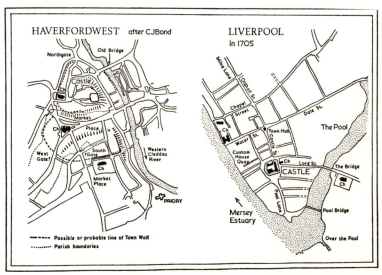

Fig 20 Town plans of Haverfordwest, Pembrokeshire, and Liverpool, Lancashire (in 1705). Attempts to trace the medieval town wall at Haverfordwest have met with little success so far. At Liverpool the medieval street pattern around the castle site was laid out on a peninsula adjacent to the Pool

When choosing a site to settle, man generally takes the line of least resistance within the limits of his technical abilities; thus if the land is easily drained, low-lying areas will be settled in preference to higher, more remote ground. For instance, at Cirencester much of the Roman town was sited on marshy ground, where the skill of the town builders was sufficient to keep the site dry. Subsequently, when the technical competence of the inhabitants deteriorated, marshy tracts of land were generally avoided. Only in Victorian times was the Watermoor area of Cirencester resettled with artisan housing. Man has tended, therefore, to choose a well drained site with a nearby source of water. Steep or inaccessible slopes have generally been avoided, although some towns sited for defensive reasons may be situated on hills or use slopes as part of their defences. An example is Malmesbury, Wiltshire (Fig 21), where there appears to be a clear distinction between the area occupied by the original Saxon town and the extended area of the later defended medieval town.

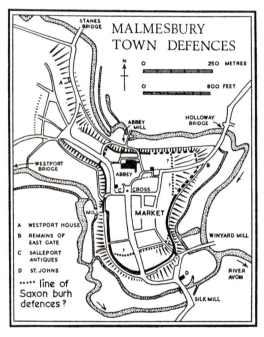

Fig 21 Malmesbury, Wiltshire. Plan of probable town defences based on breaks of slope. The Saxon burh apparently occupied the level rectangular area between the two arms of the Avon. The medieval town seems to have been somewhat larger

Despite these geographical and geological considerations, we must not ignore the human element. Nature provides the site, but man chooses it according to his own needs and against the background of his cultural and technological achievements. In the early Middle Ages defence was a major consideration, though once the need for defence is past, a town may decline both physically and economically. The medieval towns at Caus Castle and Richard's Castle in the Welsh borderland appear to belong to this category (Fig 22). Prof Beresford describes the former, which is now an

Fieldwork in Towns

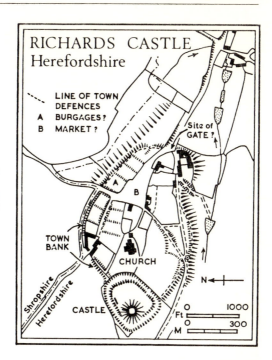

Fig 22 Richard's Castle, Herefordshire. Plan of the earthworks of the deserted medieval town. Adjacent to the large motte and bailey are traces of the burgage tenements, streets and market place of the town surrounded by a prominent defensive bank

enormous overgrown rambling earthwork, as 'a prehistoric monster crushed beneath the weight of its own armour'.[9] In both cases there is a considerable area of surviving earthworks, clearly demarcating the plan of the former town.

A clue to the original site of the town may be provided by changes in ground level or breaks of slope still visible in the townscape. They may be more permanent than other features in the street plan or pattern of property boundaries, and can occasionally reflect the location of structures which occupied the site before the town was established. Within urban areas land has tended to rise gradually because of the accumulation of refuse, and therefore there may be abrupt changes of level along town walls or boundaries as well as between different parts of the town. Warwick is a good example of this, for sharp breaks of slope and change of level can be used in association with other evidence to trace the line of the medieval town walls (Fig 23 and plate, p 103). A record of minor breaks or

Fieldwork in Towns

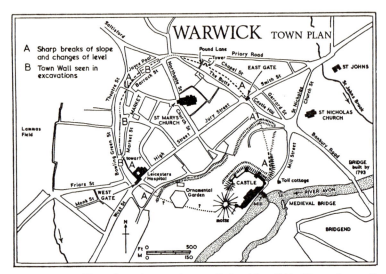

Fig 23 Warwick. Town plan with course of town wall plotted from field evidence and excavations. The construction of a park around the castle from the seventeenth century onwards led to the destruction of much of the southern half of the town and the diversion of the river crossing from the medieval bridge to an eighteenth-century bridge farther upstream

changes of slope on large-scale maps may provide much background information concerning the layout of the town: possible lines of defence, the extent of early occupation on the site, and even information about the positions of buildings such as churches or religious houses. Contour plans of towns can be valuable, particularly if the contour intervals are of 1m or less.

TOWN PLAN

The basic street plan, particularly that of the smaller provincial town, tends to be a feature of considerable antiquity, dating from the time when the properties and roads were first laid out. This date need not necessarily coincide with the foundation of the town, but it will reflect some period of planning associated with new or renewed urban activity. Until recently, when for the first time many ancient town plans have been radically altered to accommodate the motor car, street alignments tended to remain comparatively static. Indeed town plans as recorded on the nineteenth-century first editions of large-scale OS maps often bear more resemblance to the medieval townscape than do modern maps to the nineteenth-century plans. The eighteenth-century map of Liverpool (Fig 20), for example, shows the siting of the original town on a promontory, and a relatively simple street pattern centred on the castle, but this form has been effectively masked by subsequent redevelopment.

Historians and geographers have been aware for many years of Georgian and Victorian town plantations and planned extensions, and we are all familiar with towns planned and developed on new sites in the twentieth century.[10] But now it is clear that the planned town is the norm in urban settlement at any period, and that towns of organic origin are rare. This does not mean that after a town was created it did not subsequently grow organically, but often there remained some degree of supervision in the form of its growth.

The simplest and most manageable features are straight roads and rectangular blocks of land. It is not difficult, therefore, to recognise surviving elements of grid patterns representing periods of former planning in most British towns.[11] Most towns of Roman, Saxon and medieval date contain elements of town planning in the form of regular street layouts and property boundaries. After the Norman Conquest there was a spate of town plantation. This was the work of territorial lords, kings, barons, bishops and abbots, and was a specialised aspect of the well known multiplication of boroughs by seigniorial grants to old established villages.

Many town plans have indications of their earliest planned layouts within them, and the study of such topographical features can provide useful historical information in the absence of documents or excavated material. If we take, for example, the medieval towns of the Oxfordshire region, it is quite obvious from their plans that they were originally planted. Although some of the towns have documentary evidence to confirm this, for several their plan provides the only surviving evidence (Fig 24).

Separate phases of planning can often be recognised in town plans even before the extensions of the eighteenth and nineteenth centuries. Bristol and Lincoln provide two good examples (Fig 25). At Bristol a number of well defined elements of urban extension have

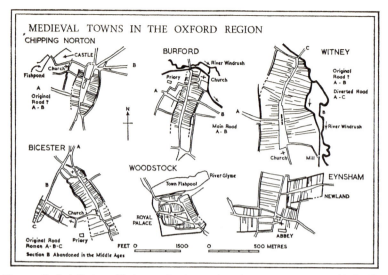

Fig 24 Oxford Region. All these medieval towns have documentary or topographical evidence indicating that they were planned settlements. There is evidence of the diversion of roads into the towns of Chipping Norton, Burford, Witney and Bicester. The isolated siting of the churches at Chipping Norton, Burford and Bicester argues for their existence before the towns were laid out

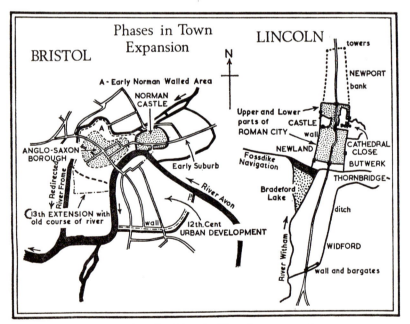

Fig 25 Bristol and Lincoln. Phases in town expansion

been identified, including the addition of the twelfth- and thirteenth-century suburbs to the south of the Anglo-Saxon and Norman boroughs. At Lincoln, apart from the two principal elements of the Roman city, there was a large ditched suburb to the south called Widford and an embanked suburb to the north called Newport in the Middle Ages. There appears to be evidence of similar developments at Nottingham and Hereford (Fig 26), and almost certainly at Oxford (Fig 27) and Northampton (Fig 28), where several phases of expansion can be identified. It may well be that when one planned element was completed, as the town prospered another section was added and developed to continue the town's expansion, sometimes in a different form or on a different alignment.

The arrangement of burgages or town plots within any section of the built-up area may help in the understanding of the town plan by indicating which were the more important roads and where there were originally back lanes. We know little of the comparative size of tenement plots between one town and another, or how size and shape were related to various parts of the town's plan at different dates. The width of the traditional 'burgage' plot may deviate from the basic 15ft and the size of plots may vary from old successful towns to new planted towns: in the latter the plots may have been larger to act as an incentive to settlement. In some new towns the plots themselves may have been placed directly on to the strips of old open fields. Certainly the shape of the burgages at Stratford-upon-Avon, Warwickshire (founded 1196),[12] and Thame, Oxfordshire (founded c 1150),[13] seems to suggest an open field origin. The tenements appear to be in the form of a reversed S, the characteristic shape of medieval ridge and furrow (Fig 29). The original town plots may, however, have been subdivided longitudinally or transversely, a small area may have been detached or added later, or several plots may have been combined to form a larger property. In some towns where documentary evidence is particularly abundant it is possible to trace the changing fortunes of individual plots over 600 or 700 years, as, for example, in Oxford and Canterbury.[14]

We shall now consider some specific aspects of the medieval town plan. Despite the fact that there were well over 100 walled towns in

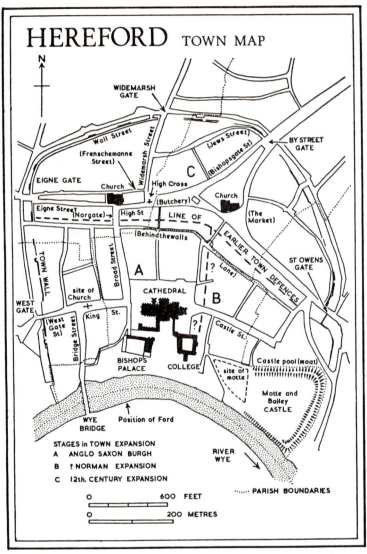

Fig 26 Hereford town map. At least three main phases in the development of the town plan have been recognised from archaeological, historical and topographical evidence

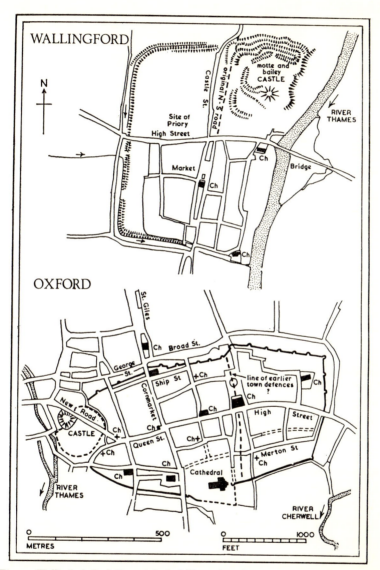

Fig 27 Wallingford, Berkshire and Oxford. Town plans of two successful Saxon burhs. At Wallingford the ramparts surrounding the Saxon town can still be seen, with a large Norman motte and bailey castle overlying the north-east corner. Little trace of the Saxon defences at Oxford has so far been found, although there is a medieval town wall and a pattern of probable Saxon streets

Fieldwork in Towns

England and Wales in the Middle Ages, only a handful have been adequately examined.[15]

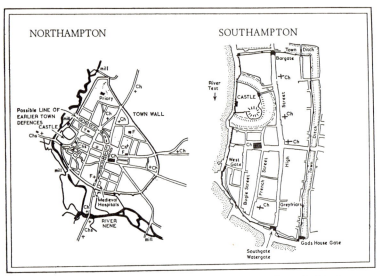

Fig 28 Town plans of Northampton and Southampton, Hampshire. At Northampton an earlier line of town defences can be distinguished and the street pattern is of a regular planned nature. Southampton is a late Saxon planned town with an intrusive castle

Defences

One of the main reasons for the creation of many towns was defensive. The need to secure centralised administration and trade was a factor in later Saxon England leading to the founding of dozens of fortified centres. In the late ninth and early tenth centuries Saxon kings created a series of planned defended towns known as *burhs*, from which the word 'borough' is derived (Figs 21, 26 and 27). These formed part of a master plan according to which the whole of southern England was crossed by a line of fortresses, and these represented the first planned towns since the Roman period. At places such as Chichester and Colchester these *burhs* often used Roman fortifications while employing a new street plan. In other places, such as Wareham, Wallingford and Cricklade (see plate, p 85), the defences and street plans were laid out for the first time. These early urban defences were mainly earth and timber, but after the

Page 103 (above) *Warwick. Subsidence cracks in a house built over the town ditch. The house on the right, at a higher level, is situated within the medieval town up against the line of the town wall;* (below) *Wantage, Berkshire. A cruck-framed building encased in later brickwork and refronted in the twentieth century. Note the bottom of one of the cruck trusses in the centre of the photograph*

Page 104 (above) *Old Radnor, Radnorshire.* Oblique air view of the shrunken village. A castle ringwork and the church in its circular churchyard remain, the extent of part of the original village boundary is marked by a curvilinear hedge, and there is an area of rather indistinct earthworks in the field to the west of the church; (below) *Merton, Oxfordshire.* Filled aisle arches and a former roof line can be identified on the north side of the church. The population of the parish appears to have declined at some time in the late Middle Ages. A large area of earthworks nearby indicates the site of a nucleated medieval settlement

Norman Conquest stone walls and ditches became normal. The fashion for town defences declined during the later Middle Ages, but walls were kept in repair in many towns right up to the Civil War in the 1640s.

Whatever the original physical form of urban defences, they were extremely important in the development of town plans. Originally most town defences were designed as an integral part of the plan, but at a later date they often provided a physical barrier to expansion. When the original defended area proved to be too small, the town either expanded beyond the walls or new walls were built to encompass the larger area. The walls were often of considerable length, those at Norwich, York and Chester being $2\frac{1}{4}$, $2\frac{3}{4}$ and 2 miles respectively. In some cases, however, the medieval defences were designed to protect an area of land much larger than the town itself, and accordingly there was ample room for subsequent expansion. Shrewsbury and Wallingford are examples.

Apart from differences of ground level reflecting the former presence of town defences, physical evidence may survive in the form of gates, towers, stretches of walls or earthen banks, or, less conspicuously, as remains of masonry incorporated into the back of properties. Few medieval gates have survived, since their main function was to obstruct traffic, and they were often removed in post-medieval times when their defensive function had lapsed. However, a number of roads heading to one point can often indicate the former existence of a gate or access through the town defences, as, for instance, at Leicester and Northampton. Towers and bastions survive only occasionally, and even then they may be completely enclosed by later buildings, but lengths of wall frequently formed property or parish boundaries and often survive as such today.

Parallel roads originally separated by the defences of a town may be recognisable even when the defences themselves have disappeared. Such roads often run either side of the site of a wall, as at Warwick, Nottingham, Oxford, Ipswich, Southampton and Pontefract (Yorks). These parallel roads may also indicate the existence of hitherto unsuspected defences, as, for example, at Hereford and possibly Northampton, where parallel streets within the later medieval walled

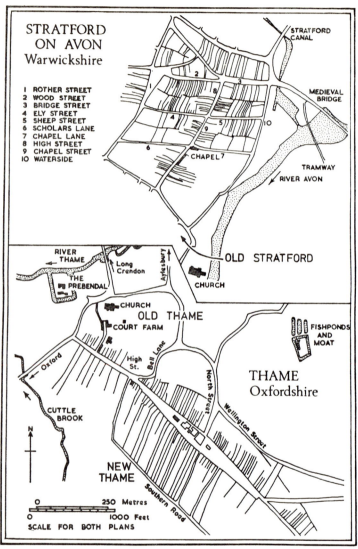

Fig 29 Stratford-upon-Avon, Warwickshire, and Thame, Oxfordshire. Plans of medieval planted towns. Stratford was established by the Bishop of Worcester away from Old Stratford in the twelfth century, probably on four blocks of land in the open fields. Thame was laid out in the twelfth century by the Bishop of Lincoln adjacent to the old village around the church. The Bishop obtained licence from the Crown to divert the Oxford–Aylesbury road into his town, a course which it still takes

Fieldwork in Towns

town have been proved by excavation to mark an earlier line of defence. Another frequent indication of defence works is roads ending for no obvious reasons as cul-de-sacs, for once they may have ended against the line of the town defences.

Sometimes all traces of medieval defences have disappeared and any attempt at identification has to rely purely on topographical information. Take, for example, Haverfordwest, where no above-ground evidence for the walls survives and the attempt at reconstruction shown in Fig 20 is speculative. One possible hint in such cases can be given by buildings which have partly subsided into an underlying ditch system. In such cases houses often develop cracks or even eventually collapse. The plate on p 103 shows how severe cracking has developed in a house built over the south-western section of Warwick's town defences.

Castles
Castles do not appear in England until after the Norman Conquest. In the Saxon towns the castle was therefore superimposed on to an existing plan or occasionally built outside the old defences. In towns built after the Norman Conquest, however, the castle formed part of an integrated town plan.

Castle precincts have been particularly important in influencing town plans. The shape of a bailey cutting across the regularity of a town's plan may be evident from circular peripheral roads. This is particularly noticeable in Saxon towns that had a later Norman motte and bailey or ringwork castle added, such as Warwick (Fig 23), Wareham (Dorset), Wallingford (Berks) and Oxford (Fig 27). Usually the rounded defences of the castle contrast with the rectilinear shape of the town's plan.

Towns which were established within castle baileys, particularly garrison towns in Wales and the Welsh border, have street patterns that mirror the earthwork defences. These are often irregular although the settlements must have been planned deliberately. There are examples at Tonbridge (Kent), Pleshey (Essex), Devizes (Wilts), Richmond (Yorks), Richard's Castle (Fig 22) and Kilpeck (Fig 1). The garrison town consisting of a motte and several baileys, one of

Fieldwork in Towns

which may have had a civil settlement within it, may indeed have given rise to many topographical elements in small towns and villages all over the country. To sum up, a castle may have been an integral part of a town's plan or a later addition which could and often did involve considerable disruption of the town and its inhabitants. The Domesday Book supplies many examples of houses being thrown down to make way for the construction of a castle in the immediate post-Conquest period, for example Shrewsbury and Oxford. In some Welsh towns the castle, town plan and town defences were conceived and built as one, as at Caernarvon and Flint (Fig 30).

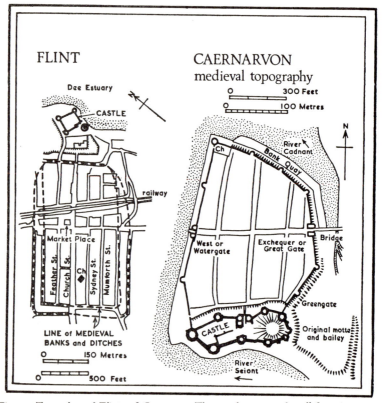

Fig 30 Town plans of Flint and Caernarvon. These settlements can be called garrison towns. They have grid-iron street patterns and constricted areas of building surrounded by elaborate defences. Both were founded, planned and fortified by Edward I

Market places

Although many medieval towns prospered without either wall or castle, none were able to survive without trade, and this was normally centred upon the market place. In many towns the medieval market place was the focal point, and the pattern of roads and tenements reflect this.

In Saxon *burhs*, in which defence was a major consideration, no permanent market areas appear to have been provided within the town plan. Trade was presumably carried out in churchyards and open areas inside the town defences. In the early Middle Ages an extra-mural market would have been developed, or an area may have been cleared within the town for a market. At Oxford there is archaeological evidence to suggest that Cornmarket Street was widened in the Norman period to accommodate a market within the walls, though the main market area of St Giles was completely outside the defended town. At Warwick and Wallingford too properties appear to have been cleared to create central markets (Figs 23 and 27).

In the early Middle Ages there was a close relation between the church and market place, and in many cases, as at Newport (Salop), the church occupies a central island in the market. There was often a connection between saints' days and the days of local fairs. Weekly markets were often held on Sundays until the late thirteenth century. The Statute of Winchester (1285), however, ordered that 'henceforth neither Fairs nor Markets be kept in Church Yards for the Honour of the Church', and the creation of a considerable number of town market places appears to date from this time.

The market was a trading place where town and country people congregated, but it was also a place of supervision and regulation. A number of well defined market shapes were designed to meet these needs. It was necessary to provide sufficient space for free movement within the market area, while at the same time making access and exit points small enough to be controllable and suitable for the collection of tolls. The long rectangular open area is a common form, while funnel and triangular-shaped market areas are frequently found in southern and central England. A less common, but more striking form is the bow-shaped market area. Long rectangular open areas can be seen at Clare, Suffolk (Fig 40) and Chipping Norton, Oxfordshire (Fig 24); funnel or triangular-shaped areas at Hereford (Fig 26), Ely, Cambridgeshire (Fig 32) and Woodstock and Bicester, Oxfordshire (Fig 24); and bow-shaped open spaces at Thame, Oxfordshire (Fig 29) and Marlborough, Wiltshire.

In many towns there is more than one market area and they are often of different shapes. Sometimes, however, it is difficult to pick out medieval areas; more often than not there will have been some encroachment or infilling which will have changed their shape. The entrance to old markets may be distinguished by a concentration of roads. With the aid of a large-scale map the fieldworker should be able to distinguish the old market frontage from subsequent infilling. In some respects it was a logical process for canvas stalls to be replaced by tiled *shoppa*, as the lord of the market, whether king, seigneur or burgess, saw that it was in his interest to have permanent rather than temporary market stalls.

Encroachments consist of blocks of buildings occupying part of or even all of the old market area. These buildings rarely possess gardens or closes, and are usually separated from the old market frontage by a narrow lane. In Hereford (Fig 26) two large market areas appear to have been almost completely infilled. All Saints' Church originally occupied an island in a rectangular market running from the Eigne Gate to the High Cross, but infilling has reduced this to two narrow, roughly parallel streets. A triangular market nearby occupied the north-east area of the town below the By Street Gate. The whole of the centre of this area has been infilled. The markets thus extinguished appear to have been replaced by streets of specialist traders such as the butchers in Butchers Row. Later some livestock markets moved right outside the town centre.

Streets and roads
The fieldworker should try to identify on the ground the older streets in a town. The rear of properties in many towns is often demarcated by a back lane, often called just that, by which goods and sometimes animals could be taken in and out of the tenement without

passing along the High Street. The arrangement of the main roads, side roads and back lanes should accordingly be examined in great detail. Later improvements to earlier plans may be obvious, or it may be possible to trace them from documentary evidence, but the possibility of earlier alterations should also be considered. These may have involved the removal of one or more properties to provide an access road, or a by-pass may have been developed around a steep hill.

Prehistoric trackways, drove roads and Roman roads may later be incorporated into town plans, as at Ludlow in Shropshire (see plate, p 86), Alnwick (Northumberland), and Montgomery. Sometimes these roads betray their origins by their incongruous relation to the rest of the town plan; but alternatively, they may have been one of the reasons for the town's foundation, and thus have been integrated into its plan. At Warwick the town was laid out at the junction of a valley route following the Avon with a cross-country route fording the river there (Fig 23). This formed the basis of the later street pattern. A similar situation exists at Worcester on the River Severn (Fig 31).

Some street and road patterns can be explained only by the present, or former, existence of a ford or bridging point which has been moved, as seems to have been fairly common (Fig 26). Dead-end roads, awkward right-angle bends and *cul-de-sac* settlements can result. The names 'Bridgend' or 'Bridgetown' are common where a small extra-mural settlement has grown up over a crossing opposite the main town, even if the bridge has long since disappeared. Examples of this are to be seen at Warwick, where the bridge toll-house is incorporated into an extant building next to the site of the ancient bridge, and at Totnes, Devon (Bridgetown Pomeroy, see plate, p 35) and Dorchester-on-Thames, Oxfordshire (Bridgend).

Any change in direction of roads or lanes within a town, no matter how slight, may be significant and any abrupt change requires explanation. Slight anomalies may reflect the joining of two separate phases of town development. There may also be features which have now disappeared from the townscape but whose influence is still reflected in the street pattern.

Fieldwork in Towns

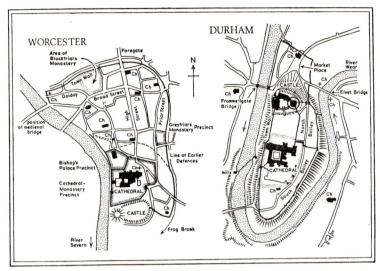

Fig 31 Town plans of Worcester and Durham. Worcester Cathedral was initially established in the seventh century. In the Middle Ages ecclesiastical precincts of various types occupied much of the walled area. At Durham, an eleventh-century foundation, almost the whole of the defended area was occupied by the precincts of the castle and the cathedral

Precincts and boundaries

Precincts defining the limits of ecclesiastic or manorial boundaries within a town plan can persist over a considerable period of time, since they are often reflected in boundaries or street alignments. Monastic and cathedral properties, palaces and even graveyards can be considered here. For instance, Wells Cathedral precinct is clearly demonstrated by two rows of houses built for Vicar's Choral about 1348, and on either side are the houses of cathedral officers such as the Master of the Fabric, Archdeacon and Chancellor. In some towns the dissolution of religious houses within the town provided space for urban expansion, but frequently the form of the precinct was preserved. The probable extent of the precinct of the Greyfriars, Worcester (Fig 31), can be traced partly from surviving remains and property boundaries.

Most Saxon and medieval towns had far more churches and chapels than are evident today. Although these will often be very difficult if not practically impossible to detect from field evidence alone, where known they may provide explanations for parts of a town's layout or the siting of some property boundaries. Parish boundaries can also survive over long periods, although there is a tendency for these to be forgotten and for the significance of walls or their boundaries along the ancient limits of the parish to remain unappreciated. At Warwick the line of the eastern town wall was formerly mirrored by the parish boundary (Fig 23), and at Hereford (Fig 26) the line of former town defences is accurately reflected by a parish boundary north of the cathedral.

BUILDINGS

Medieval buildings do not generally survive in their original condition in towns, since many are renovated over the years and others are knocked down. In periods of prosperity, buildings tend to be replaced or at least refaced, and thus early complexes can be destroyed or completely masked by later buildings. Within any property different parts tend to have different survival rates. Fronts of buildings on the ground floor are altered mostly as shops are rebuilt or functions are changed. At the back, alterations may not have been so radical.

The large number of ordinary buildings that make up a town have by and large been very little studied. They are related to plot or property sizes, and thus display a variety of shapes and arrangements, both in plan and elevation. Many towns possess some medieval buildings, but because of the later practice of encasing early buildings in brick or of refronting them with stone or brick façades, the real date of a building may not be apparent from the street frontage (see plate, p 103).[16] Before starting work, the fieldworker should familiarise himself with the main types of early urban buildings in order to understand the fragmentary remains he is likely to find.[17] He should also try to acquaint himself with the different building materials and styles to be found in any particular town. Tentative chronologies can easily be constructed to indicate periods of activity or prosperity, although these will vary considerably from region to region. At Lavenham (Suffolk) the wool prosperity of the later Middle Ages is expressed in finely carved timber halls and merchants' houses, stone in the form of flint being used only in the magnificent church. In contrast, at Chipping Camden (Glos) similar wool prosperity of the same period can be seen in the fine late-medieval Cotswold limestone houses.

In towns the church and main buildings of monasteries did not often survive the dissolutions of 1536 and 1539 unless they were made into cathedrals (as at Gloucester and Chester), but the smaller buildings were often retained and used for domestic purposes, as at Abingdon (Oxon) and Evesham (Worcs). It is often difficult, therefore, to determine the arrangements of buildings within a precinct without excavation. Churches can give useful clues to a town or parish history if they are correctly interpreted, and even the position of nonconformist chapels, nineteenth-century Gothic churches and later monastic houses should be studied.

Secular buildings such as townhalls, guildhalls and market halls usually occupy central positions, whereas institutions such as courts, prisons, lock-ups, schools, hospitals and workhouses may be almost anywhere. Much of the later history of a town will evolve around these buildings, and some at least may have retained their original functions. Their positions are often of little significance, since many were built wherever a plot of land became vacant. However, many 'hospitals' and/or almshouses of medieval date were situated near town gates, where travellers could stay overnight after the gates had been shut at curfew.

The eighteenth century saw the first real expansion of towns on any scale, although before that there had been development of workshops and houses behind frontages. In some cases this form of growth continued until areas of land were released from agricultural use in the eighteenth and nineteenth centuries, but the subsequent planned expansions have received little attention until recently.

The fieldworker should record old workshops, warehouses, factories and buildings whose function has now obviously been altered; and should look for old advertisements, blocked arches and windows, and hoists remaining on the front of buildings, all of which may be an aid to understanding. Much of this approach is detailed in books on industrial archaeology.[18]

NAMES

Names, especially those of streets, can give useful if sometimes confusing information. Many of them are more permanent than buildings, but if they have been altered several times in a town's history the documentary references may be difficult to correlate with physical features. Specialised market names, such as Bull Ring, are often retained and are of value in reconstructing the function of such areas within the town plan. The common name 'Shambles' or the earlier 'Fleshshambles', usually indicative of a meat market, comes from the Old English *scamel*, Latin *scammelum*, meaning a little bench. Some names such as 'Newland' [at Eynsham (Oxon, Fig 24), Pershore (Worcs), Whitchurch (Salop), Banbury (Oxon) and Cogges-by-Witney (Oxon)] indicate newly settled land, usually urban in character. The names Old Town [Stratford-upon-Avon (Worcs, Fig 29) and Brackley (Northants)] indicate the earlier village from which the town has developed. Street names may also indicate phases of a town's development: for instance, Old Street, Ludlow (Shropshire), and the many New Streets, as at Deddington (Oxon), though the latter are often contemporary with the town's medieval foundation and not new at all.

Street names often indicate former occupations and hence the status of particular areas of a town. 'Rother', 'Chipping' and 'Shambles', as well as simple 'Market' names, indicate places or streets where general markets were held. Specific types of market are indicated by such names as Cornhill, and Cornsteading (London and Ottery St Mary); Cornwall (Leicester); Bore-Hill or Bawdey Hill and Butcher's Row (Shrewsbury); and Butchery Lane, Draper, Mercer's Row, Woolmonger Street, Wood Hill, Horse Market, Sheep Street and Mare Hold (now Mayor Hold) in Northampton. In Pontefract, for instance (Fig 32), a remarkable collection of commercial trading names round the church of St Giles represents the infilled market place west of the medieval town.[19]

Groups of foreigners are revealed in place-names such as Petty France (Westminster), French Street (Southampton, Fig 28), Danes Gate (Lincoln), Fleming Gate (Beverley), and also in the forms

Fieldwork in Towns

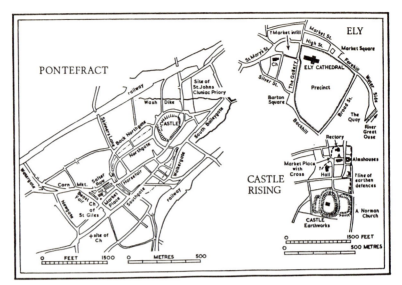

Fig 32 Plans of Pontefract, Yorkshire; Ely, Cambridgeshire; and Castle Rising, Norfolk. Pontefract originated as a castle-borough but developed around an extra-mural market place by the church of St Giles. Ely is dominated by the Cathedral precinct; the town surrounds a surviving market square and a western infilled market area. Castle Rising is a decayed town and port, which lies next to the castle earthworks; parts of its street pattern and possible defences can still be traced

Jewry or Jury, indicating the whereabouts of the medieval Jewish quarter.

Names may indicate defences as well, as in Walfurlong in Tamworth (Staffs) and Walditch (now Joyce Pool) in Warwick. Gate names can be useful in the south of England but in the north the name often means a 'road' or 'way', and hence some care is necessary in their interpretation.[20]

Notes and references to this chapter begin on p 188

CHAPTER 6

Fieldwork in Villages

For the majority of people in England until well into the nineteenth century the village was home. The study of village shape, form and distribution is therefore of fundamental importance to an understanding of the rural settlement pattern. The fieldworker should remember, however, that the village, like the town, is a complex social organisation, and that there will be many questions which cannot be solved by fieldwork alone.

Of the thousands of villages and hamlets in Britain, only a small minority have been studied in any depth. These settlements, therefore, offer the fieldworker a rich area for original research. Over the past 25 years much attention has been focused on the study of deserted medieval villages by local and economic historians, geographers and archaeologists. Before this the study of surviving villages had largely been the preserve of geographers working on village forms and settlement patterns. Now, with the widening in scope of the work of landscape historians and the general adoption of the concept of medieval settlement studies rather than merely that of deserted medieval villages in isolation, a new approach to villages and their forms is required.

What is a village? In some parts of the country it may consist of no more than a small cluster of houses, while in others it may reach the proportions of a small town. Administratively the village is the community in the parish to which the parish church is attached; any other settlement, even if it is much larger, is nominally at least only a hamlet. In this chapter, however, we are concerned with ancient nucleated rural settlement in all its forms. In recent years many villages have been expanded as commuter settlements, though generally this development has taken place outside the ancient village centres and will not concern us here.

As with other aspects of fieldwork, the study of villages involves careful and concise observation accompanied by accurate recording of information on a plan, and, as always, the fieldworker should ask questions before, during and after his work in the field. Using the OS 25in maps as a base, he should add information concerning the dates and types of buildings, boundaries, breaks of slope and earthwork features. He should then examine his plan for patterns or anomalies in the arrangement of features. For example, why does this road turn at right-angles around the rectory garden? Why does the church stand so far away from the present village? What does that row of regular but rather curious cottages mean?

The following questions should principally concern the fieldworker as he looks at his village:

1 Why is the village where it is?[1]
2 What is the present arrangement of buildings, enclosures, roads and greens, and why is the village in this present form?
3 Is it possible to date the present form of the village and its various features?
4 What evidence is there of past arrangements in the village plan, and are there visible or obvious explanations for the changes involved?
5 What can be learnt of the history of the development of the settlement from the features and buildings to be observed?

Undoubtedly the fieldworker will be able to pose other questions but these should provide a useful framework on which to build a topographical study of any settlement.

THE VILLAGE PLAN

The best way to start any village study is to examine the topography of the present village. The fieldworker can then disregard obviously recent elements and mentally try to reconstruct the early village, paying particular attention to land ownership and boundaries.

The original shape and arrangement of a village will probably have depended on the physical site and the influence of some dominant authority such as the lord of the manor. The elucidation of the population changes within the village will depend on the population statistics, a good example of the use and interpretation of which can be seen in *The Midland Peasant* by Prof W. G. Hoskins (1965). In the shaping of many villages administrative and defensive considerations were combined. There may be evidence of a manor house, often moated and of elaborate proportions, or manorial buildings such as dovecotes and tithe barns. A sophisticated form of fortified manor was the castle, from which much of the administration of medieval England was carried out. Defensive considerations certainly seem to have been important to the inaccessible villages of the Welsh borderland where, for instance, most settlements possess small mottes, ringworks, or motte and bailey castles (Fig 33). It may thus be possible for the fieldworker to find traces of defended villages next to earthen castles.[2] In the case of Old Radnor (see plate, p 104) the church and shrunken village lie next to a ringwork. There is some documentary evidence to suggest that following the Norman Conquest there was widespread destruction of settlements in the Welsh borderlands and possibly large parts of northern Britain, and in some areas many villages appear to have been rebuilt close to a castle, often within an outer bailey.

Local communications may have been important for the siting of a village, and the fieldworker should attempt to find old bridges, bridging points, disused fords or old trackways, which may be useful in explaining the present topography.[3] Fieldwork alone cannot tell us about the foundation and early development of most of our villages. Excavation is making it increasingly clear that the earliest Saxon settlers did not live in the nucleated villages characteristic of the later Middle Ages.[4] It is now doubtful whether the nucleated village appeared in some parts of the country until well after the Norman Conquest. If we are to understand the foundation and development of our surviving rural settlements, much more village archaeology is required.

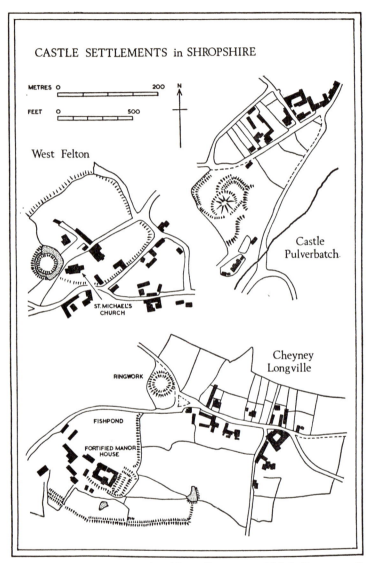

Fig 33 Castle settlements in Shropshire. These villages were established adjacent to earthwork castles, probably in outer baileys originally; all are now decayed

Fieldwork in Villages

Any attempt to classify village plans is fraught with difficulties,[5] though we can indicate certain common types which may offer the fieldworker clues to the arrangements he finds. Villages are either regular or irregular – some so irregular that it is difficult to imagine how they evolved; others regular enough to have been drawn up with ruler and graph paper. Compare, for example, the adjacent villages of Nuneham Courtenay and Marsh Baldon in Oxfordshire (Fig 34). The former was moved to its present site in 1760 along the diverted Oxford–Henley road and its creation is well documented, while the latter has no surviving evidence for its foundation apart from the plan, which strongly suggests an element of plantation.[6] The large regular green at Marsh Baldon lies some way from the church and manor house and was obviously created after their foundation.

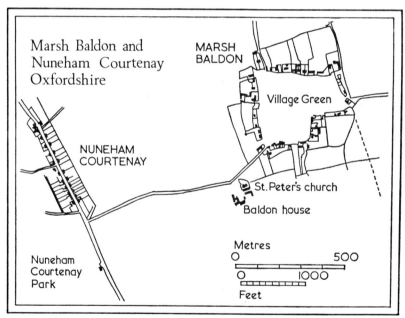

Fig 34 Plans of Nuneham Courtenay and Marsh Baldon, Oxfordshire. Both these settlements are planned villages. Marsh Baldon was probably laid out in the early medieval period away from the existing village around St Peter's Church. Nuneham Courtenay was built in 1760 after the original village site, about 1 mile to the west, had been taken into the landscaping scheme of the park around Nuneham House

Within this broad division of regular and irregular layouts we can recognise three basic types of village – those with a linear plan, those centred around a green or open space and those with a compact plan. It may be impossible for the fieldworker to categorise his village, but an attempt to do so may help to formulate the right questions about the settlement form. The village can be broken up into the following constituent elements – church, road pattern, land parcels, and greens and open spaces – which will now be examined.

THE CHURCH

The best place for the fieldworker to begin his study is with the church, for its size, character and position are of major importance. A church may have stood on its site since the remote period of the settlement's foundation, and its structure may give many clues to the development of its attendant settlements through its architecture, tombs and memorials.

Church site

The church, as the centre of village life in the Middle Ages, should logically be in the middle of the village; there are several possible explanations where it is not. Some churches were established in isolated positions, on hill tops or equidistant from neighbouring hamlets, and hence may bear little relation to any one settlement. These churches may have either been sited near a pre-existing earthwork or pagan site, or succeeded an isolated baptistry, well or spring used in missionary activities in the pre-Conquest period. Church dedications may help or hinder, since they were often altered in the Middle Ages, and daughter churches frequently adopted the dedication of the mother foundation.[7] In general an isolated church will imply some change of settlement site in the past. Most of the village will be some distance away, and there may be earthworks of the former settlement or scatters of pottery to be found near the church. Later divorced settlements are often quite regular, giving the impression that there had been a deliberate attempt to refound or develop a more rationally planned settlement away from the original nucleus around the church (Fig 34).

Fieldwork in Villages

Where the church lies within a settlement, its position should be noted and the possible implications assessed. If the church (or chapel in a hamlet) occupies a croft in a main street, it may well be contemporary with the laying out of the village. The same could apply if it is sited at the end of a main street, in the centre of the village or in some otherwise important position. If it occupies an unaligned position at the end of the village, as an odd feature in the village plan, or is unrelated to the pattern of other closes, it may well be a relict feature incorporated into a later village plan. The difference between the alignment of the village and the east–west alignment of the church may sometimes offer an explanation.

There are a few settlements, such as the Aldwincles (Northants) and Barfords (Oxon), which possess two parish churches. The reason for such an apparently illogical state of affairs may arise from the fact that there were originally two settlements sited near each other which eventually grew together. This feature of 'twinned' villages, which is particularly common in north Oxfordshire and Northamptonshire, would well repay further study.

Churchyard

The churchyard can offer a great deal of information if its features are examined systematically. Its shape is important – it may be merely one croft of the village or of no clearly defined shape. If it is circular or oval, it may be possible to interpret this as part of an earlier earthwork of a settlement or ritual site – in the west of England and in Wales a 'lan' or monastic enclosure (or cemetery) later developed as a medieval churchyard (see plate, p 104).[8] Where the boundary consists of an old stone wall or has upright stones, this should be noted, as these may have belonged to an early or pre-church monument. In the nineteenth century many churchyards were expanded, and it should be possible to determine this from changes in direction of the present wall, from earthwork remains or abrupt changes in date of burial in the churchyard extensions.[9] However, earlier changes may be evident from the casual finds of skeletons in building or trenching activities outside the present churchyard.

Fieldwork in Villages

A new area of research involves the study of gravestones as a source of local historical information, though it is only for the period c 1600–1900 that we have such potentially complete information on local populations. The gravestone with its inscription could be compared with skeletal material, and in most cases this information could be correlated with what is known of the life of the deceased from documents and parish registers. The removal of gravestones from their position over the grave represents a potential threat to information for the fieldworker in the future. From the little work that has been completed so far, it appears that, as one might expect, not everyone mentioned in parish documents is represented in the churchyards; more surprisingly, however, many persons with gravestones, including some with important monuments, are not mentioned in the registers. There is a rich area of study here for the fieldworker and demographic historian. With the increasing number of redundant churches, it is particularly important that proper care is taken to record these monuments.[10]

Church plan
Relatively little attention has been paid to church plans and their place in landscape studies. It is possible to identify certain basic church types, Fig 35 showing the main ones likely to be encountered. The fieldworker should look for the following points when examining a church.[11]

Cruciform plan churches often occur in association with 'minster' names, dedications to Saxon saints, or known missionary activity in the pre-Conquest period. Some have surviving Saxon architectural features. They may represent churches founded in isolated positions to serve a wide area rather than a single settlement, or they may have been originally relatively large and built at an early period in association with the following of a particular saint. An example is to be found at Minster Lovell (Oxon), where a large cruciform church, rebuilt by the Lovell family in the fifteenth century but presumably based on an earlier plan, is still dedicated to the eighth-century Mercian St Kenelm.

Three-part churches of nave and chancel, with a tower in the centre, often

Fieldwork in Villages

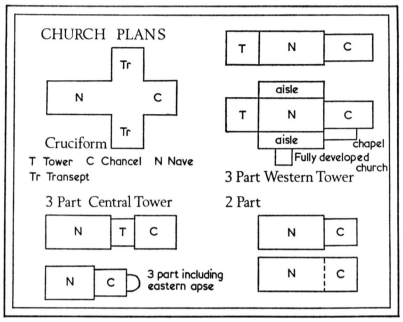

Fig 35 Church plans. The main types of church likely to be encountered by fieldworkers in England and Wales

contain late Saxon or early Norman work and such a plan, even though the main architecture may be later, may indicate an important church of the eleventh or twelfth centuries.

Three-part churches of chancel, nave and western tower with later developments, including aisles, porches and chapels, represent the typical medieval village church. They were normally manorial churches built by local lords in the early Middle Ages. The western tower was frequently a later addition.

Simple nave and chancel churches often occur in remote, agriculturally poor areas. Sometimes these will reflect settlement expansion into marginal areas in the early Middle Ages (as at Heath in Stoke St Milborough parish, Salop, or Heighington in Rock parish, Worcestershire), or churches or chapels built cheaply in the medieval period. In either case aisles, transepts or chapels were never built into them (as they were with the majority of medieval churches), a poverty of design probably indicating a static population or a relatively poor settlement unable to invest money in its church.

At the dissolution of the monasteries (1535-40) some settlements managed to retain part or all of a monastic church for their own use. Sometimes whole churches were retained, as at Tewkesbury (Glos), Hexham (Northumberland) and Malvern (Worcs); in other cases only small parts were kept, often resulting in rather odd church plans, as at Blanchland (Northumberland), Pershore (Worcs) and Wymondham (Norfolk). Traces of the monastic precinct may also have survived in the village plan.

The church building

Churches often reflect population changes in the community they serve: additions and extensions usually indicate population expansion, while demolished aisles, filled arch-aisles or even the complete demolition of parts of the body of the church may indicate substantial population decline (see plate, p 104). Similarly the simplicity or grandeur of the decoration in a church can suggest the level of wealth of the lord or the community. In many Cotswold churches prosperity from the wool trade is reflected in elaborate church decoration. After a careful analysis of the church's architecture and of its internal features it is often possible to offer a tentative outline of the periods of prosperity, demographic pattern and philanthropy evident in a settlement's history. The fieldworker should remember that the survival of ancient architecture in the form of Saxon[12] or Norman arches, or of decorations such as wall paintings, tombs or monuments, is in fact in most cases evidence of *lack* of improvement, money or development, and that the completely developed church could possibly have had all its earlier features buried, encased, destroyed or removed.

ROAD PATTERN

The fieldworker will need to decide if the road pattern is regular or not, and whether it is related to the local relief of the village. It is necessary to remember that the regularly attended roads of today with specific widths and cambers are not an original feature of villages, and that previously trackways wandered over the available public open spaces and frequently altered course in bad weather to avoid mud and potholes. The main road through the village may have been the only true thoroughfare, the others being merely lanes or open spaces between plots. The fieldworker should be aware of the disappearance of some lanes, and should look also for back lanes behind the crofts. Similarly, at all periods, there has been encroachment on to central open spaces, side lanes or back lanes that will inevitably blur a regular village plan. The fieldworker will need to take special note of any abrupt changes of direction in street or road. *Culs-de-sac* may have been merely access roads to fields, waste or meadow land, or they could indicate roads terminated or diverted for the creation of a park or as a result of enclosure. Other apparently dead-end roads shown on the maps may in fact continue on the ground as abandoned trackways in the form of earthworks or holloways (Figs 4 and 41). Field boundaries can also mark the sites of forgotten roads.

LAND PARCELS

There has been little study of the form and disposition of land parcels in surviving settlements, although the croft, toft or earthwork house-platform is recognised as an important element in deserted medieval villages. The fieldworker should attempt to record whether such parcels are arranged in regular or irregular rows around an open space or otherwise dispersed, whether they are embanked or ditched, and what material their boundaries are made of. Similarly their length, depth and size, and also their relation to ancient roads and paths, will need to be considered. Normally there will have been considerable amalgamation, sub-division or alteration of sizes and shapes of parcels, so that it may be difficult to distinguish the original arrangement. However, old internal divisions and small linear earthworks may provide clues. Excavation on deserted medieval village sites has tended to suggest that boundaries between properties were in some cases very fluid and ephemeral.

Some land parcels within the village enclosure can be identified as special units. We have already considered the churchyard as a case in point, but there may be others formerly occupied by the sites of castles or monastic houses, or rectories, vicarages and manor houses still in existence.

In many villages the land of the manor house or demesne will have been larger than the normal croft, and there may have been various adjacent closes and one or more moats. Around many of the rectories and vicarages of the eighteenth and nineteenth centuries the fieldworker may discover small areas of parkland or formal gardens occupying a larger area than a normal croft. In some cases, including the manor house which may exist in a village, the allocation of such an area as a 'precinct' may have brought about the diversion or blocking of roads and the annexation or alteration of adjoining properties.

GREENS AND OPEN SPACES

A green was probably a feature of most English medieval villages. Before metalled roads were introduced, most villages had their house frontages set far enough back to permit an open grassy space in the centre of the settlement which was used for rough grazing. There are a number of villages, however, where the green plays a particularly important part in the village plan. Much has been written in the past about villages with greens, and it has sometimes been assumed that 'green' villages date from the Saxon foundation of the settlement.[13] However, it is clear that such greens are often divorced from the church, the ancient centre of the village, and it is now thought that they may date from a period of village reorganisation, possibly in the early Middle Ages.

A useful exercise would be to take a group of 'green' villages and to ask the following questions: what size are the house frontages, what percentage are farms, what is the axis and size of green, what is the position of the green in relation to church and manor? In this way it may be possible to build up a typology of greens and interpret them more effectively.

BUILDINGS

Next to the church, the manor house was the most important building, although there is no recognised position for it within the village plan. It is usually difficult to be certain that the present manor house is the same one, or is on the same site, as that referred to in medieval documents. Indeed most surviving manor houses in villages are not medieval at all but date from the seventeenth, eighteenth or even nineteenth centuries. There can be more than one manor house in a settlement, and again it is usually difficult to correlate the existing buildings with earlier documentary references. In a number of cases the manor house was moved outside the village during the Middle Ages.

Sometimes no manor house remains, but buildings which were the prerogative of manorial or rectorial owners may stand in the shape of dovecotes and tithe barns. Such buildings could also have been attached to monastic granges in villages.[14] It is difficult to date dovecotes, although, generally speaking, the circular examples appear to be earlier and are often medieval. They were certainly built and used for pigeon breeding from the twelfth century to the nineteenth.[15] Sometimes they are obscured by other farm buildings, or they may survive as low earthen or circular hollow mounds. Tithe barns are generally recognisable by their size and monastic or church-like appearance, or by elaborate timber roofing structures, but, like dovecotes, large barns were also built after the medieval period. Field names sometimes help in the location of tithe barns, as do general building surveys in a village and the study of documents.

Another factor to look for is the relation between buildings and their attached land; if they occupy the street frontage, have only a narrow passage down the side, or are sited gable-end to the road, this may indicate that the village had urban aspirations. Most of the buildings surviving in any village, however, will be ordinary vernacular dwellings, and the fieldworker should find out their approximate dates. Farmsteads and farm buildings are usually evident in villages, especially if enclosure was carried out rather late in the eighteenth, or in the nineteenth, century, and although they may be no longer utilised as farming units, barns, stables and various other agricultural buildings will probably remain.

It is often extremely difficult to date a building from documents.

Frequently deeds do not exist, or where they do, little useful structural information is given, and the fieldworker should again rely on the visible physical evidence as his main source. Dated features are usually of some use, but date plaques or datable sculptures or mouldings can be moved, and material from other structures may be incorporated into a building. The plate on p 153 shows a cottage at Castle Acre (Norfolk) which has fragments of medieval masonry incorporated within it but was itself probably built in the eighteenth or nineteenth centuries.

Although much can be learnt from an exterior examination of a building, far more can be understood, both of its date and original arrangement, if the interior is studied. The fieldworker should attempt by means of a sketch map to understand the layout of the building under consideration. Which parts, for instance, are definitely later additions, which walls are new, which doorways, windows and staircases have been added or removed? All these questions should be posed. The basic two or three unit plan, one room thick, persists from the medieval period to the seventeenth century, and even encasement or rebuilding in the sixteenth and seventeenth centuries has not usually obscured such a plan where it exists. The hall was usually accompanied by a solar or private room, a kitchen and a service room. Variations on this theme are numerous, but it is common all over the country.[16] The position of the chimneystack is important. Before the improvements in comfort in the sixteenth century, buildings had no stacks. They were usually added either at the end of the hall against the screen passage near the service rooms or on an outer wall of the hall. The most fruitful area for examination is the roof space, where carved or blackened timbers may indicate that the house was open to the roof in the medieval period, although such evidence may be completely masked by improvements downstairs.

Notes and references to this chapter begin on p 189

CHAPTER 7

Fieldwork in the Countryside

The British rural landscape offers the fieldworker his richest area of exploration, yet attempts to understand patterns and features in the countryside are comparatively recent. Although individual parishes and regions may have been studied in some depth,[1] the fieldworker's chosen area will probably have previously received scant attention. It is true that large-scale maps record the buildings, roads and fields, and it is possible to reconstruct recent past landscapes with some degree of accuracy,[2] but they do not record the subtle earthwork structures and relations within the countryside with which we are primarily concerned in this chapter. The fieldworker should look at a parish or region as a whole, and examine village and fields together.

DESERTED TOWNS AND VILLAGES

Considerable impetus both to British medieval archaeology and landscape studies has come from recent work on settlements, especially deserted villages. Much of this work has been stimulated by the Medieval Village Research Group (formerly the Deserted Medieval Village Research Group). Despite this work, which has revealed the existence of thousands of abandoned settlements in this country,[3] many areas, particularly in the west and north, remain unexplored. The Medieval Village Research Group classifies a site as being deserted if it has a church, manor house and farmhouse – a maximum of three standing buildings. The conditions of deserted villages vary considerably; in some cases they have been ploughed out completely (see plate, p 153)[4] or covered by modern buildings,

Fieldwork in the Countryside

while in others the enclosures, roads and dwellings of the old settlement may be clearly identifiable as earthworks (see plate, p 154). A useful rule of thumb classification as to the state of the earthwork has been produced by the Medieval Village Research Group in the form of the following code. Such codes can naturally be adapted for the recording of earthworks other than those belonging to deserted villages.

Code indicating visible quality of sites

A*   Excellent. (Very good pattern of roads and crofts with house-sites visible, eg Wharram Percy, Yorks, ER)
A   Very good. (Pattern of roads and crofts, but no house-sites visible, eg Hamilton, Leics; Quarrendon, Bucks)
B   Medium. (Good street or streets but otherwise confused earthworks, eg East Tanfield, Yorks, NR)
C   Poor. (Vague bumps making no certain pattern, or church ruins without visible earthworks, eg Stoke Mandeville, Bucks)
D   Nothing to see at all at known site

Whatever the state of the earthworks it is probable that the site has never been surveyed, although it may have been seen and possibly photographed from the air. In these cases the fieldworker has a ready-made task in producing as informative a ground plan and record of the site as possible.

To some extent the fieldworker's approach will depend on the amount of work already carried out in any particular area. If he is studying a previously unexplored region, he will have to start by identifying the sites, but if a number of sites are already known, his principal task will be to complete the pattern in order to produce county or regional plans of deserted settlements and make a record of them.

Identification of sites

There are three main techniques to be considered here. Firstly, the fieldworker should start with the OS 1in map, which will give an immediate impression of the regional settlement pattern. He should then look for obvious anomalies, perhaps the most important being parishes with churches standing in isolation. As already explained, there are several reasons why a parish church may lie apart from the community it serves, the most common being dispersal or desertion of a settlement. If upon visiting the church the fieldworker finds that it contains architecture of any antiquity (pre-1700) or if there is any indication, for instance a Norman font, that an older church originally stood on the site, he should examine the surrounding fields for traces of holloways, house platforms and ridge and furrow.

The presence of blank areas on the map or parishes without a central village must also be investigated, because they often reflect settlement abandonment. Prof Beresford has demonstrated the use of this technique to locate a series of deserted medieval villages in the Midlands.[5] Fig 36 shows a similar situation on the Oxfordshire-Warwickshire border. An alternative to this is to look for points at which tracks or paths converge for no apparent reason: they may meet on the site of a former settlement. Similarly the extensive plotting of ridge and furrow within the area, followed by an examination on the ground, may lead to the identification of deserted villages, moated sites or parks. In the parish of Ducklington (Oxon), for instance, the application of this technique led to the discovery of three previously unknown deserted villages, one moated site and a medieval park (Fig 37).

Secondly, known medieval archaeological features can also lead to the identification of sites. Deserted villages and sometimes even deserted towns often lie next to castle sites, their features dwarfed by the defensive earthworks or stone structures of the large monument. Occasionally such settlements lie within the area of an extended outer bailey or hill fort, as appears to be the case at Castle Camps, Cambridgeshire (Fig 38). Alternatively an extension to the castle may have obliterated the village, and in such situations the castle may partially cover the earlier village earthworks, as at Hen Domen (Montgomeryshire). A moated farmstead or fishpond indicated on the map may also mark the site of an adjacent medieval village, and should be visited to see if there are any associated earthworks. In-

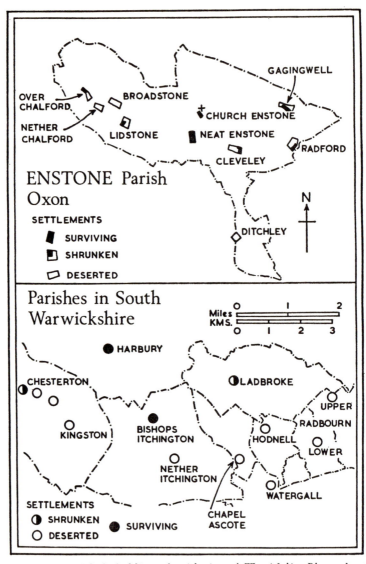

Fig 36 Enstone parish, Oxfordshire, and parishes in south Warwickshire. Plans such as these help to show the density and distribution of medieval settlement and to some extent explain why parts of the modern landscape appear so empty

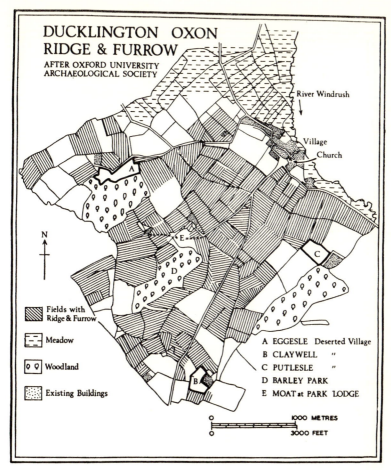

Fig 37 Ducklington, Oxfordshire. A map of the ridge and furrow in the parish emphasises land use in the medieval period and explains several of the blank areas – three shrunken hamlets, a park and a moated-lodge site

deed rural sites rarely exist in isolation and should be seen as elements within a wider pattern.

Another way of identifying deserted villages is the aerial photograph. There are a considerable number of prints within the national repositories of archaeological aerial photographs showing deserted medieval village sites. These have yet to find their way into any

Fieldwork in the Countryside

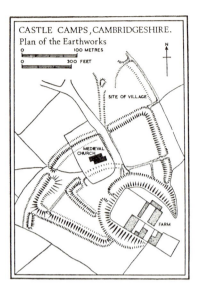

Fig 38 Castle Camps, Cambridgeshire. Plan of the earthworks around the church. Here there is a large ringwork now occupied by a farm, several baileys, part of the site of a medieval village and possibly earlier earthwork features

catalogue or publication, and for all practical purposes the sites remain to be discovered. The reader will no doubt be familiar with classic deserted medieval village air photographs, but often he must be content with much more modest evidence. Even quite faint irregularities may mark a former occupation site, whereas apparently good earthworks may cover nothing more than an area of old marl quarrying;[6] only excavation or experience in dealing with the different forms of earthwork configuration will solve this problem.

As a general rule the more pronounced the earthworks, the better the photograph is likely to be. Given a series of good photographs, it may be possible to plot the site as effectively as from the ground, though the fieldworker should always visit the area whenever possible to check details, and indeed to examine the state of the features. Although these sites are often known to local farmers, their significance is sometimes not realised, and they may be destroyed without their true importance being appreciated.

The third approach to identifying sites can be used in association with aerial photography, and involves intensive fieldwalking in order to build up a detailed picture of a parish or area. In this case it is

Fieldwork in the Countryside

possible to distinguish the probable former settlement sites from an intimate knowledge of local geography. By observing ancient features such as boundaries, holloways and ridge and furrow, one may find the former settlement simply emerging as a negative space in an area otherwise covered by traces of former cultivation.[7] One important technique of identification, which falls outside the scope of this book, is the use of documentary sources. Unless an area has already been well researched, or the fieldworker has a knowledge of medieval documents, he should be wary of this approach, since documents, more than the landscape itself, are open to misinterpretation. If he is not conversant with medieval palaeography, the fieldworker should try to find an individual or group already working on the documentary evidence for his area, and cooperate by trying to identify on the ground sites which are known to exist from documentary sources.

Recording a site

Having found a hitherto unknown deserted village, or when visiting one which has not been previously surveyed, the fieldworker should attempt to make some record of the site. He needs to be equipped with an OS 25in map and a camera, and, using the techniques described in Chapter 2, should produce a sketch plan. Ideally, he should try to produce a contour survey, but this is time-consuming and rarely possible except where excavation is about to take place. Any plan, however modest, should include details of the street pattern, the enclosure boundaries, traces of houses (with interior features if visible), headlands and ridge and furrow, and other irregularities marking such features as village wells or ponds. If the fieldworker is not working directly on to an OS 25in map, he should make sure that modern field boundaries, roads and buildings are marked in order that the plan can be related to the National Grid. Fig 39 provides two examples of earthwork plans, that of Wormleighton showing the relation of the whole of the village earthworks to the surrounding ridge and furrow. At Lower Dornford the farm lies next to a small deserted settlement and appears to occupy about a third of the old village.

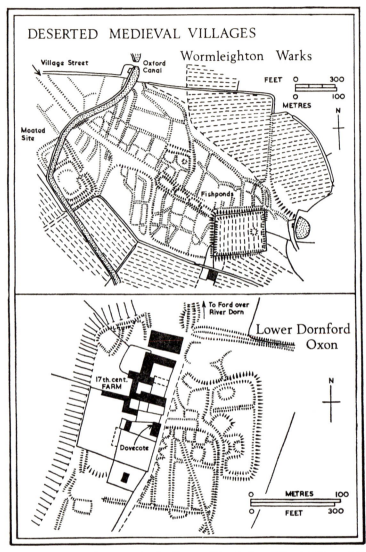

Fig 39 Plans of the deserted medieval villages at Wormleighton, Warwickshire, and Lower Dornford, Wootton, Oxfordshire. On both sites hachures have been used to depict hollow roads, house platforms and boundary banks

The Medieval Village Research Group has produced a comprehensive questionnaire (see Appendix 4), which should be completed if possible; with suitable amendments this can be employed on other types of site. It is suggested that at least three copies are made – one for personal use, one to be sent to the Medieval Village Research Group and the third to be deposited in the local archaeological archive. The questionnaire is largely self-explanatory, and the fieldworker should use the information to obtain as full a picture of the site as possible, particularly the relation between the earthworks and any standing buildings. The church is of great importance, as it is likely to enshrine the story of the development and decline of the village from the early Middle Ages onwards.

In the absence of regular earthworks, former occupation may be indicated by the presence of bunches of nettles, often in quite well defined groups. The reason is that where man and domestic animals live, waste matter is concentrated and becomes incorporated into the soil; and, long after the site has been abandoned, the local enrichment of phosphorus persists, encouraging vigorous nettle growth.[8]

Interpretation
With any set of earthworks it is possible to make a preliminary assessment of the relation of one feature with another. It may be quite obvious that structurally there are two or more phases in a deserted settlement. The village may have a clear boundary showing as a shallow bank and ditch, and this is often a useful way of determining the full extent of the settlement. If there are platforms outside the boundary, they almost certainly relate to a phase of expansion. More often, however, an earthwork site will appear to be homogeneous, in which case the fieldworker must gracefully retire, having provided his ground plan, and if the site is threatened and time allows, excavation will test his ideas. There are situations where the relations within the deserted medieval village earthworks can clearly be demonstrated, that of a castle or possibly a monastery lying over early medieval earthworks having already been cited. There are several instances where the relation between the village earthworks and ridge and furrow is of particular interest: for instance, a photo-

graph of Newbold Grounds, Catesby (Northants), taken before the earthworks were ploughed out, clearly shows that the village expanded over earlier ridge and furrow, presumably during a period of population growth or village reorganisation (see plate, p 153). Often such chronological phases are visible only from aerial photographs or detailed contour surveys.

All the features seen in deserted villages can be applied to deserted towns, though the latter tend to be on a larger scale. The principal difference is that several of them have extensive defences, within which lie the earthworks of the old town. Other features to look for include regular street patterns and burgage plots, the latter perhaps surviving as field or garden boundaries. Many sites are as yet only superficially known and a number of abandoned towns, particularly in the Welsh borderland (Figs 1 and 22) have yet to be investigated in any detail. It would be well worth examining the sites of isolated border castles for attached settlements. Even more common are towns which have decayed to the size of small villages or hamlets; they may have earthworks and relict features such as large churches and market crosses which require examining and recording.

Two examples from Norfolk are worth quoting here. The first is Castle Rising, where a decayed town and port lie to the north of the impressive castle remains. A large church containing architecture contemporary with the castle tells us something of the size of the former settlement here. An impressive market cross lies to the east of the church in the old market square, now a village green. An examination of breaks of slope, together with road and path alignments, enables the original form of the town to be reconstructed (Fig 32). Not far away at Castle Acre another decayed medieval town lies in the western lee of a great earthwork castle. The massive town defences were thought by earlier historians to be Roman, but there is no doubt that they formed part of a defensive complex contemporary with the medieval castle (Fig 40). It can be seen that the south-eastern corner of the medieval borough has been abandoned and given over to allotments, while the modern village lies in the form of a little planted unit outside the northern defences, with the wide Market Street lying partially over the northern town ditch.

Fieldwork in the Countryside

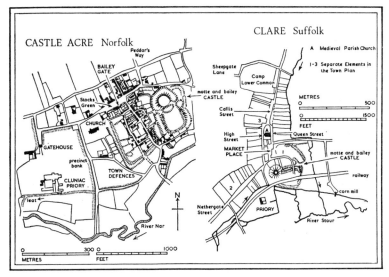

Fig 40   Plans of Castle Acre, Norfolk, and Clare, Suffolk. In both these settlements separate elements can be distinguished: at Castle Acre the castle, embanked village, church and priory precinct, and at Clare separate blocks of properties around the castle which probably indicate distinct phases in town development

Several other East Anglian castles also appear to have possessed such associated settlements. Possible sites for examination are Chipping Ongar and Raybridge (Essex) and Haughley and Orford (Suffolk). A useful starting point for working on these settlements is to be found in Prof Beresford's *New Towns of the Middle Ages* (1967).

Shrunken or shifted villages are also far more common than is generally realised. A considerable number of extant villages have associated earthworks. A survey of Northamptonshire deserted settlements records some twenty-two shrunken settlements and concludes: 'If ever a complete survey is achieved, these shrunken villages will probably emerge as the commonest English earthwork of any type or period.'[9] According to the accepted definition of a deserted medieval village, the distinction between a deserted and a shrunken village can sometimes, therefore, be a very fine one.

It is of the greatest importance that a full record is made of this type of site, particularly as so few have ever been excavated; as

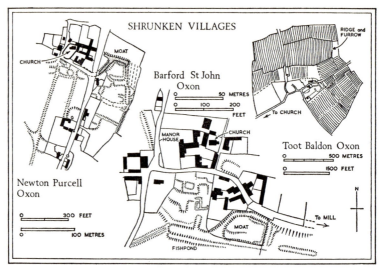

Fig 41 Plans of shrunken villages in Oxfordshire. Areas of earthworks indicate that these settlements were once much larger, although in each case several buildings survive

they are rarely recognised, they are the more likely to be destroyed without investigation. Fig 41 shows some examples from the Oxfordshire region. When examining this type of earthwork, note the position of the church particularly, as it is likely to occupy one of the oldest sites in the village. Recent fieldwork on the western extension of the M40 from Stokenchurch to the Waterstock Crossroads identified a shifted village at Tetsworth (Oxon); the earthworks of the medieval village lay along a ridge next to the church, formerly a chapel of Thame, and the modern village, complete with green, lies some way to the north along the line of the A40 road. Excavation undertaken before the motorway was constructed demonstrated that the village had moved from its earliest site by about 1300, and had gradually migrated down to the present road alignment during the later Middle Ages.[10] Further work in the area revealed an almost identical site at Lewknor, where the old village had a very clear perimeter boundary, together with a main street and associated enclosures. The plate on p 171 shows another Oxfordshire shrunken village site at Somerton, where a large field of earthworks includes a post-medieval mansion site and formal gardens adjacent to the present village.

To produce a balanced picture of medieval settlement in any one area, it is essential to identify and plot shrunken village sites, and also those associated with more obvious desertion. The surviving, shrunken and completely deserted sites in the parish of Enstone (Oxon) are recorded in Fig 36, making up the complete medieval settlement pattern. Of the ten original hamlets, only two survive as such, five are severely diminished in size, and three have disappeared altogether. However, deductions about population movements from the evidence of shrunken village or indeed deserted village earthworks alone may be very misleading if no account is taken of compensatory building elsewhere. Parliamentary enclosure, in particular, encouraged the building of farmsteads in the midst of the newly enclosed fields; while some of the village farmsteads were then used as labourers' cottages, others decayed, leaving the familiar earthwork enclosures. Similarly, the emparking movement would create model villages in one place and leave the marks of deserted house sites elsewhere, with no fall in the total population.

MEDIEVAL AGRICULTURE

Ridge and furrow
The corrugated surface appearance of many fields, or ridge and furrow as it is generally known in England, has for long been a topic of considerable interest to students of agricultural history[11] (see plate, p 171). Despite this, comparatively little intensive work has been carried out on the nature, distribution and dating of ridge and furrow. Here we are not concerned with its origins and formation, but with its special distribution and relation with other archaeological features. It is, however, now generally accepted that broad curving ridge and furrow running in many different directions is a legacy from open field farming, while the narrow straight ridge and furrow is normally related to nineteenth-century agricultural improvement schemes. In parts of the country the open fields continued in use until the eighteenth or nineteenth centuries, and it has been

demonstrated that in some manors the fields were reorganised on one or more occasions, but in such cases any surviving ridge and furrow will obviously not reflect the medieval arrangement.[12]

Ridge and furrow is best seen in areas of permanent pasture which, in the Midlands, may not have seen a plough for four centuries. In dry seasons the humped back of the former ridges is accentuated by parched grass, while the furrows remain green; in ploughed land its presence is shown by bands of different colouring in the soil or crop (see plate, p 18).

If each unit, from furrow to furrow, marks the single strip of the open fields, it is often possible to relate the earthworks to the pattern of strips as they appear on pre-enclosure maps.[13] Ridge and furrow which can be seen to be older than existing hedges has the reversed S or 'aratral' (plough) curve, and the frequent changes of direction characteristic of 'furlongs' can be accepted as the physical remains of medieval strips. The absence of ridge and furrow is, however, inconclusive, for a field may once have lain in strips that have been obliterated by subsequent ploughing, or it may never have been ploughed in strips. Apart from the fact that the ridge and furrow nearest the village is likely to be the oldest, it is only possible to date the system when other earthworks or disturbances of known date have interfered with it.

Ideally the fieldworker should try to produce a comprehensive survey of ridge and furrow within a parish or region plotted on to an OS 6in map. If this is done by fieldwalking and the use of aerial photographs, a clear pattern of the areas of past agricultural activity often emerges (Fig 37). The ridge and furrow should be plotted as accurately as possible to show any curves or other characteristic features. The mid-point trough of the furrow should be drawn into a base plan and the apex of the ridge can be dotted in. Field notes should record the height of the ridges above the furrows (highest, lowest and average), the relation of the ridge and furrow to the natural lie of the land and field boundaries, and the drainage conditions in the furrows (are they damp, for instance?). Most important of all, what is the relation between the ridge and furrow and any archaeological features?

Lynchets

Medieval lynchets or terraces appear to represent the adaptation of ridge and furrow to steep slopes, and this phenomenon is to be found throughout southern England at least. A similar recording technique to that used with ridge and furrow should be employed, and the relation with any ridge and furrow or other archaeological earthworks should be closely noted.

CASTLES

The fieldworker will encounter fortified residences in towns and villages and in complete isolation throughout the country. They range from simple motte and bailey castles to the stone fortresses of kings and lords at the height of their rivalry and power, and include the elegant country residences of the late fifteenth and sixteenth centuries that had lost virtually all military function.

The early motte and bailey castles are especially numerous in the Welsh borderland, where almost every village possessed one. At their most simple they consist of a conical mound with an attached defended enclosure or enclosures. Owing to their size, such mounds, which are normally marked on the map, are sometimes incorrectly described as 'tumuli'. Indeed it is sometimes difficult to distinguish large burial mounds from castle mottes, and undoubtedly a number of the latter remain to be discovered. The presence of a bailey, or of some remains of it, is of course conclusive, and this is the first thing to be looked for; however, some castle mounds, especially Welsh ones, never had baileys, so that their absence proves little. There are also some natural features which resemble castle mounds, and in some cases genuine mottes have been contrived out of them; scarping could be emphasised to increase the steepness of the slope. There is often valuable traditional evidence such as a field name which embodies the element 'castle' or 'camp',[14] and in such cases it is normally safe to assume that the associated earthwork is not a tumulus. Many of the lesser castles will not have been surveyed and the only plan of these is likely to be published in the county *Victoria History*, vol 1,[15] unless the area has been covered by the RCAHM. There will, however, almost certainly be an elementary plan on the OS 25in map. It is possible to use this as a base on which to add features such as outer defences and associated settlement earthworks; in many cases these will have escaped attention in the past and they are certainly worth surveying. Another feature to be looked for is a possible approach road, either in the form of a holloway, a terrace on a hillside, or a causeway in low-lying marshy areas. If the castle is near a spring or river, signs of holloways may be seen leading down to an ancient bridging or crossing point. The top of the castle mound is normally flat, unless it has been disturbed, most likely by stone robbing. In stony country the tower would have been stone-built, and remains of masonry may be visible round the edge of the platform.

When studying larger castles, the fieldworker should look for previously undetected defences or traces of water systems, as has recently been done for Kenilworth Castle, Warwickshire (Fig 42).[16] Sometimes it is possible to imagine the original form of such water defences. It may also be possible to distinguish traces of earlier defensive earthworks which have been utilised by the medieval castle: for instance, the castle at Church Brough (Westmorland) is set within the remains of a Roman fort. With all castles the relation with any extant settlement should be noted. For example, does the general settlement pattern conform to the castle layout, or does it appear to have developed independently at a later date? In particular, is there any trace of a market place outside the castle gates, either in the form of an earthwork or infilled? An open area in front of the castle gate was the natural place for a market or fair under the supervision and protection of the lord, and in the commonest plan for a village dependent on a castle the houses stand around a market place or along the sides of a broad street leading to the gates.

MOATED FARMSTEADS

The moated manor or farmstead is common in those counties where water can easily be obtained and where clay is available to line ditches in order to hold water. A well preserved example will consist of a broad wet ditch large enough to be a serious obstacle, and normally surrounding a rectangular area of about 60m × 75m. This

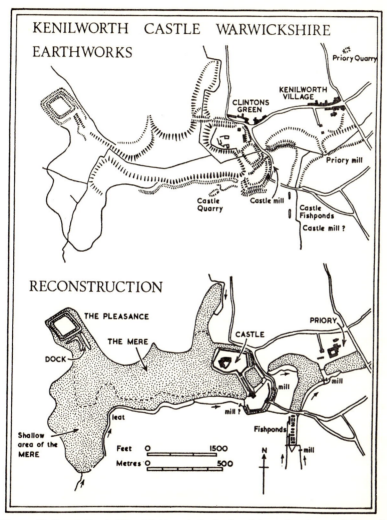

Fig 42 Kenilworth Castle, Warwickshire. A sketch plan of the earthworks around the castle and the priory enables a reconstruction of the water system in the medieval period to be attempted

area may still be occupied by a house, often of considerable age and interest, but many of these sites have long been deserted. They may be situated in the open country or in villages, and in the latter case their moats may have been partially back-filled, and are accordingly more difficult to identify. Those in open country often carry coppices or spinneys with dense undergrowth, which makes examination difficult. The presence of a square of woodland in an otherwise treeless area may lead to the identification of such sites. Sometimes there is a series of adjoining moated sites; the principal moated site may have carried the dwelling house, while the subsidiary moats enclosed farm buildings, stables, stockyards, gardens and orchards. Sometimes a moat is found in association with fishponds or, more rarely, a watermill.

The fashion of surrounding a farmstead with water continued long after any defence was necessary, so that further evidence would be needed to determine that a moated building necessarily occupies a medieval site.[17] Even in authenticated cases the building within a moated area may well have been reconstructed or re-aligned. The absence of water does not mean that a moat was always dry, as the later piping of spring water and the laying of field drains may have robbed the moat of its water supply, or the feed channel may simply have been diverted. On grassy or wooded islands there is often little to see of the medieval farmstead, even when it has not been replaced by a later building.

The former existence of moated sites can often be deduced from such features as old dog-leg fragments of wet ditch, frequently associated with copses. A visit to the site will often reveal traces of the remainder of the moat. The names of fields, woods and copses can also help with identification, for the name of a site recorded in early documents may persist even though its form may have undergone alteration. On tithe and estate maps the word 'moot' often refers to the site of a hitherto unrecognised moated farmstead. For example, the field name 'Moat Meadow' on the 1838 Tithe Map of Hanbury, Worcs, led to the discovery of a previously unknown site. In the Midlands moated sites are generally to be found in areas of early medieval colonisation, and often carry characteristic clearing names such as 'brant', 'green', or 'assart'. Where moats have been completely back-filled and ploughed over, they readily show on air photographs because of the depth of the soil in the wide buried ditch. The plans of moated sites can vary considerably and it has been suggested that oval layouts may predate the Norman Conquest. Fig 43 shows a number of plans of moated sites in the Midlands,[18] giving some idea of the variety of forms, together with associated earthworks of shrunken settlements and fishponds.

The fieldworker should look carefully for the system of waterworks feeding the moat; this may consist at its most simple of a leat from a stream, with an overflow channel returning downstream. On the other hand there may be an elaborate complex of moats, mills and fishponds. Evidence of water control in the form of sluices should be identified. This category of medieval earthwork lent itself to later landscape designers, and moated sites are often to be found incorporated into parkland schemes.[19] Thus, in areas where moated sites are known to occur, a useful start could be made in identifying new moats by examining areas of parkland. In parts of Britain the moated site is by far the most common type of medieval settlement; examples are shown in Fig 44, which illustrates identified moated sites in Tanworth and Ullenhall parishes (Warwickshire). There is little doubt that a considerable number of these sites remain to be discovered and planned. Recently a Moated Sites Research Group was established,[20] and about 2,000 moated sites have now been identified in Britain. An example of a completed record card, together with a questionnaire, is given in Appendix 5.

FISHPONDS AND MILL SITES

During the Middle Ages streams and brooks were of the greatest importance, providing a source of almost constant power to turn mill-wheels and water to replenish fishponds and eel beds. In Castle Rising (Norfolk) the parish boundary has a long narrow projecting tongue following one bank of a stream, and at the end of this projection stands a mill. When the parish boundaries were established, it was obviously considered important that a strip of land should be guaranteed for a path and millrace to serve the mill.[21] River valleys

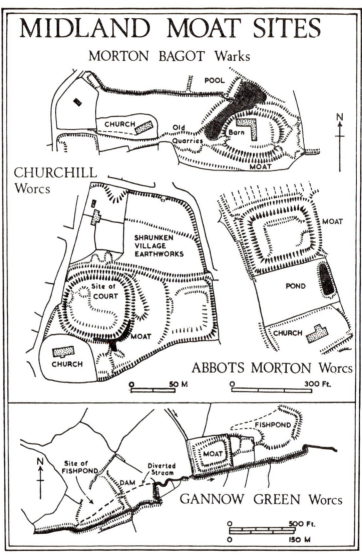

Fig 43 Plans of Midland moated sites. A great variety of moat shapes and sizes are encountered all over the country and some are shown here. Notice also the ancillary earthworks of villages, holloways and fishponds, most of which have usually not been previously recognised

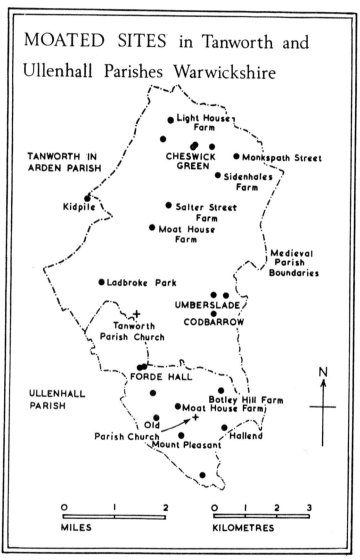

Fig 44 Moated sites in Tanworth and Ullenhall parishes, Warwickshire. This distribution of moats around isolated farmsteads represents the antithesis of the nucleated settlement pattern shown in Fig 36

Fieldwork in the Countryside

throughout the country were intensively occupied and exploited, and the fieldworker could start by taking a stretch of valley and plotting all earthworks and relict features along its length. Many of the valleys which in the Middle Ages would have been full of activity are today largely empty and overgrown. Schemes for canalising or piping water may have disturbed or destroyed medieval features, so here again there is a need to record in the face of destruction.

Fig 45 shows different types of fishpond.[22] These were normally rectangular excavations beside a small stream or spring, and are not generally found near large streams or rivers; other examples have embankments to maintain a pool of moderate depth, with either a gentle flow of water through it or a system of sluices to isolate the pond's water completely.

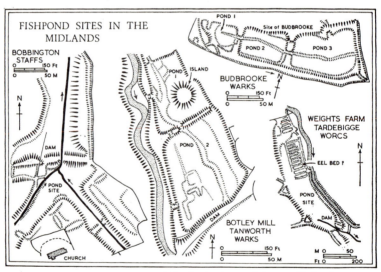

Fig 45 Plans of fishpond sites in the Midlands. A selection of the types likely to be encountered is shown here. Islands are frequently found remaining as earthen mounds, and features such as the possible eel beds at Weight's Farm can often be identified

The pond was frequently made by building an earthen bank across the line of a watercourse. One side of this bank might be stone-revetted for strength, while a sluice served to let out excess water. Where possible, the shape of the valley retained the pond, but if the

Page 153 (above) *Castle Acre, Norfolk. Fragments of carved Norman masonry built into a flint cottage which sits on the medieval town ditch. These stones probably belonged to the Norman castle or to a destroyed church or chapel;* (below) *Newbold Grounds, Catesby, Northamptonshire. Oblique air photograph of the ploughed-out earthworks of the deserted medieval village. The dark lines indicate old roads and ditches, and the light areas are patches of building material on house platforms. The area of the village is surrounded by traces of ridge and furrow*

Page 154 *Halton, Northumberland. Oblique air photograph of the earthworks of the deserted medieval village. House platforms, hollow roads, village boundary bank, and ridge and furrow are all clearly emphasised by the low sunlight. Note the size of the modern farm and its outbuildings, which cover a large proportion of the area occupied by the medieval village*

valley sides themselves were not sufficiently steep, two further embankments were often built parallel to the stream. A fourth bank upstream was sometimes constructed to complete the rectangle. In their developed form fishponds had auxiliary breeding tanks linked to them by a maze of channels and sluices, with different chambers for different types and ages of fish. Such a complex of interlinking ponds has been identified at Bordesley Abbey, Worcestershire (Fig 46),[23] where an intricate system of water management must have operated (see also pp 178–80). Not far away at Washford Mill, excavation of another fishpond complex before the building of Redditch New Town revealed traces of timber buildings, together with a woven straw pannier used to transfer the fish from breeding tanks to the larger ponds (Fig 3).

The fieldworker should begin by looking for traces of dams or banks. These have often been severely breached, but a regular unexplained break of slope across the valley floor will frequently mark the site of an old dam. Sometimes there is a series of linked ponds, and it is always worth looking for more once one has been discovered.

Watermills are found in all areas where streams can be expected to provide a sufficient constant flow of water for at least a few weeks in the year. In the later Middle Ages watermills were often adapted for functions other than grinding, such as the fulling of wool, but if only earthworks remain it will be very difficult to distinguish these functions. Abandoned watermills have distinctive characteristics – a flat building platform by the side of the stream, together with empty ponds and channels. The mill leat or race is sometimes a useful pointer to the site of a former mill; it may be a straight channel cutting off stream meanders, which often have lines of willows growing along them. In any case straight stretches of stream in an otherwise meandering course should always be examined for traces of earthworks.

Windmill earthworks are sometimes to be found either close to villages or in an exposed site in the old fields. These are characterised by a simple circular mound with an associated ditch that is sometimes mistaken for a burial mound.

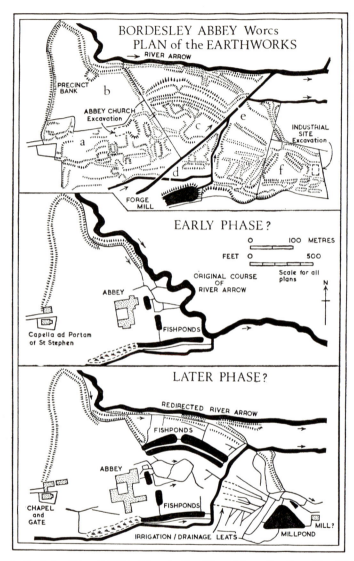

Fig 46 Bordesley Abbey, Redditch, Worcestershire. Plans of the earthworks and possible reconstructions. It will be noted that the monks probably diverted the River Arrow in order to reclaim a large area of rich meadow land in the valley. See text, pp 178-80, for further elucidation

MEDIEVAL PARKS

One of the most important elements in the English rural landscape is the country house and park. The breaking up of large parks on estates and the demolition or adaption of the country house of the twentieth century are in many ways comparable with the dissolution of the monasteries. During the sixteenth century the park changed both in form and function. Before this it was part of the lord's demesne, consisting simply of an area of woodland and pasture enclosed by an earthen bank, often with an inside ditch. The bank was topped by a wooden paling which was occasionally replaced by a quickset hedge or stone wall, and the enclosure would be broken only by gates and deer leaps. The primary purpose of the early medieval park was to keep deer for hunting; it differed from the forest, chase and warren in that it was completely enclosed. Most wealthy lords aspired to a park, which was normally some distance from the manor house.[24]

A few such parks, such as that at Woodstock (Oxon), can be traced back before the Norman Conquest, but the majority were created in the twelfth, thirteenth and fourteenth centuries. At that time the Crown issued hundreds of 'grants of free warren', which resulted in the monopolisation of hunting rights by the lord within his newly created park. In many cases deer parks were carved out of areas of royal forest.

The fashion for creating deer parks declined rapidly during the later Middle Ages, when many parks deteriorated, their boundaries being allowed to collapse and hunting often ceasing altogether. At this time some old parks were cleared of their woodland and enclosed; subsequently they were divided between freeholders or consolidated into a single farm. Thus medieval hunting gave way to a more economic land use. Heath Park (Salop), for instance, was enclosed into a farm in the mid-sixteenth century and given the name Heath Park Farm; its limits can still be traced from the field boundaries. Where such a 'park' name survives, it is usually indicative of the former existence of a medieval deer park. Earthworks relating to medieval parks are to be found throughout the country (Fig 47).

Fieldwork in the Countryside

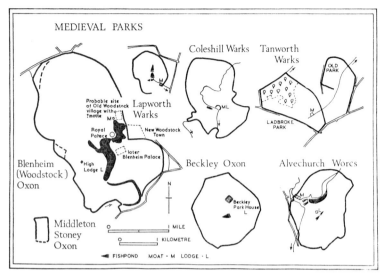

Fig 47 Plans of medieval parks. A variety of sizes and shapes of parks is encountered in the landscape; the rounded outer boundary is particularly common. Internal features likely to be found include fishponds, moated sites, lodges and deer leaps

During the Middle Ages many banks and ditches were constructed around woods, fields and villages, quite apart from parks, and these medieval enclosures can be distinguished from more ancient linear earthworks by the comparatively steep-sided nature of their banks and their well pronounced ditches. The cross-country course of a medieval enclosure bank will normally be respected by modern field boundaries.

LINEAR EARTHWORKS

In Britain there are many stretches of bank and ditch known as linear earthworks. They appear to date mainly from the Iron Age, Romano-British and Saxon periods. By their very nature they are difficult to date, but they do present the fieldworker with a positive challenge to record and possibly interpret. Their function is still not clearly understood, but they are now generally believed to have been mainly boundaries. Offa's Dyke, running from North Wales to the Severn estuary, is the most impressive of the Saxon banks, but many

Fieldwork in the Countryside

stretches of a more modest variety remain to be examined. Some of these earthworks may relate to Saxon estate boundaries. The tracing of boundaries from Saxon charters can be a particularly rewarding, if often difficult, fieldwork exercise.[25] See also pp 50–51.

MONASTIC SITES

There is little problem in identifying monastic sites, as most of them are well known. The OS map of *Monastic Britain* shows the distribution and character of religious houses in Great Britain from the eleventh century to the sixteenth. However, their granges and small dependent houses may not be so easily recognised.[26] The rediscovery of lost monastic sites and a survey of those already known will normally require the use of aerial photographs taken in dry conditions. The principal parts of the monastery may be self-evident. The robbed stone walls sometimes stand out very well and the ground plan can be compared with the known plans of the order concerned. The water channels and ponds are nearly always important, and planning these can often lead to a far greater understanding of the site. The outlying earthworks relating to farm buildings, field systems and the precinct boundary may be less well defined, and are often the most neglected aspects of the complex. A good example of this can be seen at Maxstoke Priory, Warwickshire (Fig 48). The plate on p 172 shows the outlying earthworks of Sawley Abbey (West Riding). At Bordesley Abbey (Worcs), a Cistercian foundation, a detailed ground survey shows the whole monastic complex, and from this it is possible to hazard guesses about its territorial expansion (Fig 46). A cutting through the precinct boundary suggests that the twelfth-century abbey may have been laid out on agricultural land.[27]

FIELDS AND HEDGES

The application of modern agricultural techniques in many areas of the country is currently leading to the removal of field boundaries and the creation of immense fields. The removal of these boundaries, many of them of considerable antiquity, represents the destruction of an important element of the historic landscape.

Many of the fields of the Midlands were created by Parliamentary

159

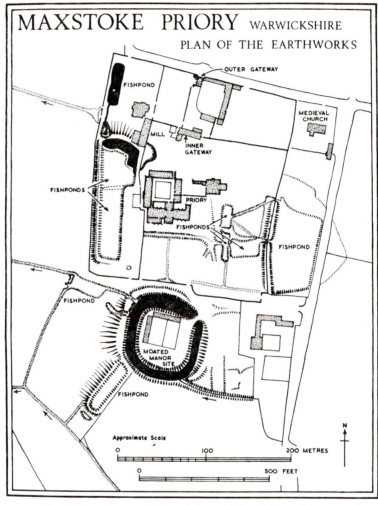

Fig 48 Plan of the earthworks at Maxstoke Priory, Warwickshire. A large moated manor site with fishponds and an area of village earthworks can be distinguished next to the walled monastic precinct. Within this the claustral buildings remain as clear earthworks and many of the medieval fishponds and water channels survive intact

enclosure in the eighteenth and nineteenth centuries (Fig 12). The characteristic features of these fields are that they are regularly shaped, with straight hedges and associated ditches. The roads that run in such areas are normally straight, with wide verges. Areas of Parliamentary enclosure contain isolated farmsteads often built of a material different from the indigenous buildings of adjacent villages.[28]

Other field boundaries are older – generally speaking, irregular fields found close to a village are early. Similarly hedges which grow on banks are often ancient. However, unless cartographic or documentary evidence exists, it is very difficult to date hedges accurately. One approach which may aid fieldworkers is that advocated by Dr Max Hooper, who claims that there is a direct relation between the number of shrub species and the age of a hedge. He suggests that, on an average of a 30yd stretch, a hedge acquires one new species every 100 years, so that a hedge with ten species per 30yd will be about 1,000 years old.[29] Although this theory may not be universally applicable, it is certainly worth trying to build up a local or regional pattern of hedge species.

MEDIEVAL INDUSTRY

The relics of medieval industry are not always easy to identify, but the sites are rewarding to look for. Much medieval industry was sited in small valleys. The principal areas of iron production were the Weald of Kent and Sussex and the Forest of Dean, but there was a considerable amount of activity in other areas where iron ore was readily available. The most important sites are known, but much work remains to be done on the identification and plotting of lesser sites.[30] The major features of this industry in the south are the many dams built to create heads of water, or 'hammer ponds'. Another result of ironworking was the creation of bell-pit ironstone mines, in which the waste material from medieval iron pits was disposed around the openings of shallow shafts leading down to the bed of ore. The shafts subsequently collapsed, leaving a hollow in the centre of the spoil heaps. Such bell-pit mines are a feature of other aspects of medieval industry, such as coal and lead mining.

Medieval stone quarries are comparatively difficult to recognise, as the quarryman was limited by the scale of his operations. He usually removed the topsoil and piled all over-burden along the side of a wide trench; he then extracted the stone suitable for building, to a modest depth, mostly by utilising natural fissures and with the help of weathering. Ancient quarrying areas are covered with open trenches, pits and rubbish mounds, now masked by grass and trees. The main problem is to distinguish these remains from post-medieval activity and, if the area has been continuously worked, this may not be possible. The course of deeply sunken trackways serving quarries can sometimes be traced and plotted.

Evidence of medieval pottery, brick and tile manufacture is well worth searching for, if only because the sites are so elusive. Such sites, particularly those of pottery kilns, are of the greatest importance, as the study of ceramics forms a major element in medieval archaeology. There is little chance of any obvious surface earthworks surviving, but spreads of pottery may be identified in ploughed fields. The fieldworker should also look for place-names containing elements such as 'potter' or 'kiln' and then visit the relevant field to seek for ground evidence.

An activity which led to the creation of interesting coastal structures was salt-making, a process involving the extraction of salt from sea water and salt-impregnated mud. After impurities had been allowed to settle from the salt solution, the water was evaporated by the sun's heat or with the assistance of charcoal and turves slowly burned around the salt pans. The collecting channels and the heaps of debris, chiefly burnt clay and ash, form the earthworks and islands known as salterns. These curious relics of the salt industry stud reclaimed marshland and fenland on the east coast of England. The accumulation of mud from which salt had been extracted was itself an agent in the reclamation of marshland, and the salt-makers were progressively driven seawards by their own industry. The hump-backed mounds of older debris soon acquired a grass cover and became difficult to distinguish from solid ground.

ROADS AND BRIDGES

Medieval roads are not particularly easy to identify, for more recent road-building has often obliterated traces of earlier routes. However, it is sometimes possible to distinguish medieval tracks, which are frequently found in association with earthwork sites such as deserted settlements and castles, and their courses can often be traced some distance overland. Often they exist in the form of green or 'hollow' ways (holloways) deeply entrenched in the landscape, or as causeways in some low-lying areas. Field roads found in areas of ridge and furrow are also quite common. Some roads can be identified from names, many of the long overland trade routes carrying names with the element 'salt', 'cattle' or 'drift'.

A considerable number of medieval bridges still survive. The actual point of crossing would be determined by favourable physical conditions, such as a narrow channel and a firm foundation in the river or stream bed, together with a good approach across solid ground. The same conditions had favoured fords, and many bridges simply represent the replacement of a ford. Where an old crossing proved inadequate, the construction of a new bridge at a different

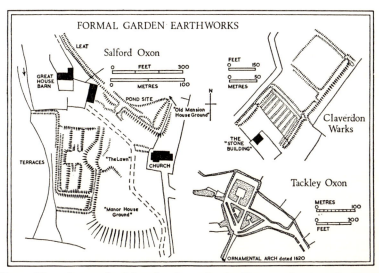

Fig 49 Plans of post-medieval formal garden earthworks. These sites date from the sixteenth and seventeenth centuries and represent terraced lawns, gardens and bowling greens attached to lost or partly destroyed mansions. The water system at Tackley is typical of the formal moats and ponds of this period

point soon diverted traffic and challenged the fortunes of any village that had depended upon the old route. Sometimes when a medieval bridge has been replaced by a later construction, the alignment of the crossing will have changed; this often results in an uncomfortable relation between the bridge and the more ancient road pattern.

There is a wide range of post-medieval earthworks which the fieldworker is likely to encounter. Apart from the earthworks resulting from industrial activity, decayed formal gardens of the type shown in Fig 49 and the plate on p 171 may be quite common. There are groups of elongated or 'pillow' mounds in parts of the country, and these look remarkably like neolithic long barrows. However, they appear to be medieval and post-medieval in date and were probably constructed for the encouragement and habitation of rabbits. They are often found near ancient rabbit warrens.[31]

Notes and references to this chapter begin on p 190

CHAPTER 8

The Organisation and Application of Fieldwork

Throughout this book the need for detailed fieldwork has been stressed, but it is equally important that the information obtained should be readily accessible to other workers. Ideally the fieldworker should operate within a county or regional structure into which the results of his work can be fed. At the moment, unfortunately, we are far from having a comprehensive system of county museums, county archaeologists or regional organisations, so that the fieldworker may have to devise his own recording system. Whatever scheme is adopted it should be readily transferable. The factual information found during fieldwork should be treated in the same way as archaeological finds, ie the find and the circumstances of its identification need to be recorded.

CARD INDEXES

To begin with the fieldworker will probably find a card index system organised on a parish or topic basis the best method of recording. This system can be elaborated as the fieldworker wishes. The card produced by the Oxford City and County Museum shows the type of information that might be included (Appendix 6). An alternative version has been produced by the Essex County Council (Appendix 7).

MAPS

There should be a complete set of OS $2\frac{1}{2}$in or, preferably, 6in maps of the area to be covered, on which the location of each site or find can be accurately marked. When dealing with areas of dense concentrations of cropmarks or finds, it may be necessary to use OS 25 in maps. Where there are a large number of maps involved, there will be a problem of map storage. There are two basic map filing systems: the plan chest with pull-out drawers or the plan cabinet where maps are suspended vertically on strips which fit on to pegs. The authors recommend the latter system for ease of retrieval of information. If the fieldworker is dealing with only a limited number of maps and plans, a simple cardboard folder will probably be adequate.

PHOTOGRAPHS

Both ground and air photographs require good filing techniques. Normally photographs are filed on a parish and county basis, but it is considerably easier to file air photographs according to kilometre grid squares. Provided that cross-references are made with a card index, either system can be used. Transparencies can also be filed by parish or topic, but if these are to be used for other purposes, such as teaching, a broader based system involving the consecutive numbering of each slide may be preferable.

A SITES AND MONUMENTS RECORD

With large numbers of cards it may be necessary to organise a fully comprehensive recording system, so that different types of information can be retrieved. The following is a description of the system employed in the Oxford City and County Museum – Sites and Monuments Record.[1] This is a highly sophisticated system, and normally far beyond the capacity of the lone fieldworker. It does, however, show how landscape information should be stored ideally and illustrates the need for a practical and logical system of fieldwork data storage and retrieval. The objectives of this record are several, including the accumulation of the divers sources of information about the physical remains of man and his activities in the Oxford Region into one manageable index, and the provision of a short cut to all other records, local or national. In this latter aspect it aims to make available for local use relevant information contained in the

The Organisation and Application of Fieldwork

two principal national topographical archives – the National Monuments Record and the Archaeology Division of the Ordnance Survey.

The record includes material of all periods, including sites and monuments relating to the Industrial Revolution. The material is divided into a number of separate units consisting of one set of index cards; a set of record maps; large manuscript plans, sections and drawings; documents files; ground and aerial photographs; and, finally, a cross-reference unit based on punched feature cards. The link between all these units is that every site or solitary find is given a unique number called the *Primary Record Number*. With the exception of aerial photographs, all records within each separate unit are arranged in straight numerical sequence, irrespective of the type or the period, the site or the find. In other words, none of these basic record units are sub-divided on a typological, period or topographical basis. Thus, for example, Primary Record 2455 represents a castle in the parish of Somerton (Appendix 6). This number will be written on the index card (*the Primary Record Card*), on the record map in the appropriate position, on any plans of the site (then stored in the Manuscript Plan Unit), on any relevant correspondence (then placed in the Document File Unit), and on all slides and ground photographs. The number given to the following site or find is simply the next available number. If new material relevant to a site which already has a number is added to any of the units, then this material is simply fitted into the numerical sequence in the appropriate storage unit.

The *Primary Record Cards* call for little comment. They are available for local fieldworkers in Oxfordshire who wish to supply information to the Museum. The procedure adopted for quoting authorities for statements made on the card follows that used by the Archaeology Division of the Ordnance Survey.

The *Record Maps* are a vital part of the record and, again, the conventions used by the Archaeology Division of the Ordnance Survey are employed to denote the varying degrees of accuracy within which a site or find can be plotted (Appendix 8). There are many instances where the location or extent of sites or finds cannot be adequately described except on a map, and the Record Maps, therefore, contain a certain amount of unique information. This system can be adapted and modified according to the type of exercise being undertaken, but the fieldworker may well find it useful to adopt these conventions in the field.

The basic Record Map is the OS 6in, and a complete set is maintained for the county. In some cases this scale map is too small for distinguishing individual sites, and OS 25in maps have therefore been used when the density of sites increases. The use of maps on this scale is complicated by the current revision being carried out by the Ordnance Survey in selected areas; as new metric maps are being published on a National Grid basis the old 25in county series are being withdrawn.

Large-scale OS 50in maps are being used to compile information for the city of Oxford. The first edition (1874) on the scale of 10in to 1 mile is also used, since the maps in this edition are particularly useful for recording medieval and post-medieval sites and monuments before much urban redevelopment took place. Useful adjuncts to the 6in Record Maps are two sets of transparent overlays for each OS 6in sheet on which are plotted surviving ridge and furrow field systems and field names.

The Documents File or the *Detailed Record File* contains more information than can be conveniently included on the record cards. This file holds correspondence, detailed descriptions of sites, small sketches, drawings, photographs and so on. Also included are details of 'linear antiquities' – roads, linear earthworks and canals. Again following the practice of the OS Archaeology Division, folders with 1in strip maps are compiled to show the extent of the course of the feature, together with notes on the history and detailed description of short stretches.

The *Manuscript Plan Unit* includes the original plans and sections of surveys and excavations carried out by fieldworkers and the museum staff.

The *cross-reference* system adopted is one based on punched feature cards. In other manual systems the problem of retrieving information about, for example, all Anglo-Saxon period material from a particular parish is generally solved by arranging duplicate cards in a series of classified indexes. The use of punched feature cards avoids this duplication and enables a greater range of features or characteristics to be isolated. The system reduces to a minimum the number of index cards or other records which have to be sorted to obtain information. The individual punched card represents not an individual site or find but features or characteristics, and the holes punched in the card represent those sites or finds which have that feature or characteristic. One card provides an index to all the sites and finds in, for example, the parish of Somerton. Another may represent all the sites and finds of the Anglo-Saxon period contained in the index. When the information on these two cards is combined, an index to all sites or finds of Anglo-Saxon date in the parish of Somerton is provided; theoretically, therefore, all sorts of finds or sites can be compared.

Aerial photographs cannot be ordered conveniently on a primary record number basis and are therefore indexed on a National Grid/kilometre square basis following the practice of the National Monuments Record Air Photographs Unit. Details of the grid reference, location, subject, date photographed, photographer, original negative number and source, and the primary record numbers which apply to the sites on the photograph are all written on the back of the print. The collection includes aerial photographs of local sites and copies of the extensive surveys in the keeping of the bodies mentioned in Chapter 4.

The index now contains over 8,000 numbered sites, monuments and find spots, and for topographical information is the most comprehensive single index for the region, although it does duplicate the main elements of the OS Archaeology Division's index. Since the Division's index utilised all the main published and unpublished sources, information from early surveys such as the *Victoria County History* inventories are covered, together with information from national and local periodicals. Systematic searches through museum accession registers and collections are needed to ensure complete coverage, although much of this has been done by Ordnance Survey card compilers. Where this material already figures on the Division's record cards, the Sites and Monuments Record provides something of an index to material in other museums' collections.[2]

All previously known areas of cropmarks – for example, at Stanton Harcourt, Standlake and Eynsham (now destroyed by gravel quarrying) – have now been plotted by members of a volunteer study group on to 25in record maps. This record helped to make possible a survey of all cropmarks between the Goring Gap and Lechlade.[3] It is now possible, therefore, to gain a picture of what has been done in the Upper Thames Valley and to determine more easily than before which sites, or parts of sites, may still be available for further work.

At a time when computer-based systems are being developed for museum collections and also for various aspects of local government administration, the requirements of archaeological and historical records also need to be considered. Moreover, since the local planning authorities in many areas are currently investigating and developing computer-based systems for planning purposes, coding of information for archaeological and historic sites will have to be worked out in order to include these aspects in planning processes, notably development control. Whatever systems are adopted, however, collection and collation of the basic data presents the largest single problem.[4] This is partly due to the lack of precision in techniques now employed.

The information the Sites and Monuments Record contains reflects to a very large extent the state of archaeological and historical work in the region, and its utility depends upon the amount of support given to it by local fieldworkers. A valuable extension of this Record would be the launching of detailed parish surveys, as has been carried out in Cornwall and other counties.[5] Eventually this would lead to a much more realistic and systematic knowledge of our historical environment.

Two case studies will illustrate the use of fieldwork involving areas of landscape which were to be badly disturbed.

THE M40 ARCHAEOLOGICAL RESEARCH GROUP

The fieldwork carried out in 1970–2 along the line of the M40 be-

Page 171 (above) *Somerton, Oxfordshire. Oblique air photograph of shrunken medieval village earthworks and terraced gardens of a sixteenth-century manor house picked out by low sunlight;* (below) *Abberwick, Northumberland. Oblique air view of earthworks and ridge and furrow. Notice the characteristic reversed S shape of the ridges mirrored in the later field boundaries and the area of earthwork enclosures in the centre*

Page 172
Sawley Abbey, West Riding, Yorkshire. Oblique air photograph showing the monastic buildings surrounded by earthworks of the medieval precinct. These probably represent agricultural and industrial buildings and enclosures. Such areas have rarely been investigated

tween Stokenchurch on the Chilterns in Buckinghamshire and Waterstock Crossroads in Oxfordshire illustrates many of the problems and advantages of detailed work ahead of redevelopment projects. When the route was known fieldwalking began under the auspices of the Oxford City and County Museum and Oxford University Department for External Studies, and in November 1970 an M40 Archaeological Research Group was established. The Group acquired detailed OS 6in and 25in plans of the line of the motorway, and all the landowners concerned were contacted and gave their permission for advanced fieldwork to take place.

The Group was divided for fieldworking into three sections to cover the 3-mile western, central and eastern stretches of the proposed route. In the winter of 1970–1 an intensive fieldworking campaign was undertaken to examine in great detail every field in a ¼-mile wide corridor south of the present A40 in which the motorway was to be built. Finds slips were prepared and details of hedges, land use and finds, together with grid references, field numbers and fieldworkers' notes were sent to the central repository at the Museum. At this stage all material was carefully examined and any archaeological or historical information was plotted on the 25in base maps. The groups were each given an afternoon's training to teach them to identify objects and fill in the finds slips accurately. Afterwards they were left very much on their own, although there was a group leader to whom they could report in case of any potentially significant find. The fields were walked on many occasions under very different conditions. Gradually significant clusters of prehistoric, Romano-British, Saxon and medieval finds began to emerge on the maps. By March 1971 the Group was in a position to point to areas of possible archaeological importance. These were normally on land which had been ploughed, but also included areas of earthworks on permanent pasture land where sub-surface information was less readily accessible.

While fieldwork was progressing, systematic work on documents, old maps and aerial photographs was undertaken to provide evidence of various sites. A map was compiled from tithe maps of the field names along the motorway route, revealing indicative names such as

'Camp Corner', 'Upper Ruins' and 'Lower Ruins', the 'Old Bury', and 'Kiln Close'. Areas of former open fields at Lewknor, Adwell and Postcombe were located, as well as the older enclosures at Tetsworth, Attington and Stokenchurch. Work on possible and probable Roman roads in the area was carried out separately. Appeals to local pilots resulted in their taking up members of the group for aerial surveys, and photographs taken regularly in the early months of 1971 provided much new information. The National Monuments Record Air Photographs Unit took a series of air photographs over the line of the motorway which proved to be of the greatest importance, since a number of previously unknown cropmark sites were identified. With the assistance of the Research Laboratory for Art and Archaeology at Oxford, three of the more enigmatic sites located by fieldwalking were examined with a magnetometer, but unfortunately the results were rather disappointing. As a consequence of this work, trial excavations were undertaken to determine the nature of cropmark sites at Camp Corner and to examine the shrunken village at Tetsworth.

As soon as contractors moved on to a site, another phase of fieldwork began. It was hoped to be able to examine the holes dug for the fencing which lined the motorway, but in this case posts were driven in mechanically. Very soon, however, drainage trenches were being put down on each side of the proposed road, revealing a considerable number of archaeological features – for example, the line of a medieval road, a late Romano-British cemetery, a Saxon cemetery and a Romano-British settlement site of unknown character. The trenches were particularly useful in areas of permanent pasture, where they afforded the first and only opportunity to examine possible archaeological features.

The next phase of interest to archaeology was the removal of all hedge boundaries along the line of the road. This time no archaeological features were revealed, but on other motorways considerable archaeological material has been found preserved within the hedge banks.

The final stage of the M40 Group's work was concerned with the scraping of the motorway which preceded major construction. In this instance several new sites, including a large Iron Age settlement, were identified and a last-minute rescue excavation was mounted.[6] Over the whole 9 mile length of the route some sixteen new archaeological sites were uncovered, and happily most of them were not completely destroyed by the motorway. Fig 50 shows the distribution of finds along the length of the motorway, together with the known sites lying in the corridor proposed for the northern extension. In the light of experience there can be little doubt that a considerable number of new sites will be revealed as soon as fieldwork starts.

RECORDING SITES IN REDDITCH NEW TOWN, WORCESTERSHIRE

New towns pose another major threat to archaeological material. In recent years, however, there has been a considerable awakening to the value of the total recording of sites within new town areas, so that the proper preservation of a proportion of sites will link the new town historically to the ground on which it is built. Usually the best way to achieve this is to preserve those buildings and monuments of interest which can demonstrate aspects of the area's history. Some new town development corporations have been enlightened enough to appoint full-time archaeologists to undertake this survey work, but in the late 1960s, when the work at Redditch (Fig 51) was undertaken, such ideas had not been fully formulated. The Development Corporation does, however, help financially and gives other forms of material assistance.

All potential help in the area was contacted and volunteers mobilised in order to try to collate as accurate a picture as possible of the town's archaeology and topography. This study was undertaken by colleges of education, schools and historical societies within the area. As with the M40, the work was divided between fieldwalking, documentary research, and the examination of aerial photographs. The main area of interest centred in the first instance on the earthworks of the Cistercian Abbey at Bordesley. A description and interpretation of the earthworks is included here to provide an example of the way such sites can be dealt with.

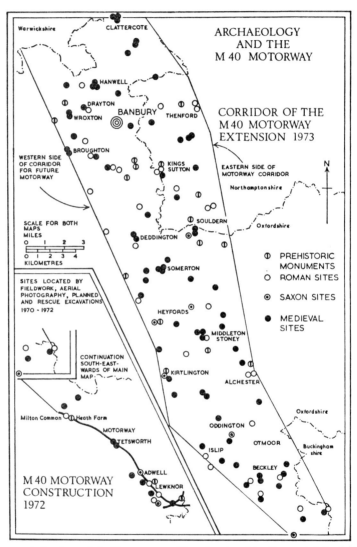

Fig 50 Archaeology and the M40 motorway. Sites of various dates discovered during fieldwork and construction in 1972, and the known sites in the corridor to be occupied by the proposed future northern extension – compiled from the Sites and Monuments Record at the Oxford City and County Museum

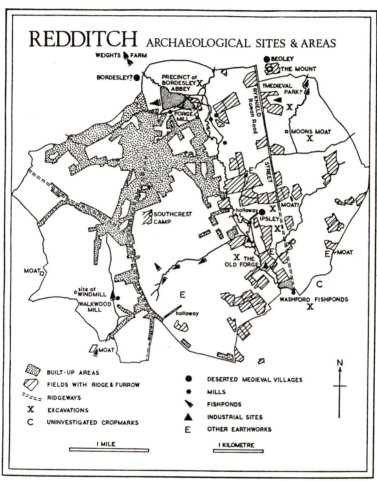

Fig 51 Map of archaeological sites and areas in Redditch New Town, Worcestershire. An example of the compilation of data from fieldwork, documentary sources and air photographs to provide a background to modern development

The Organisation and Application of Fieldwork

Bordesley Abbey earthworks
While the abbey (Fig 46) was being excavated in 1968, a full-scale survey was made of its associated earthworks along the valley of the River Arrow. Altogether earthworks were located in six different fields, and these will be briefly described before a tentative explanation is offered of the earthworks' origin and significance.

Field a, containing the main abbey remains, is known as Abbey Meadow, and by its western gate are flat platforms which probably indicate the site of the gatehouse and its auxiliary buildings. Immediately to the south of this is the small enclosure where once stood St Stephen's Chapel (in use until the nineteenth century), the *capella ad portam* of the abbey; gravestones can still be found hidden in the grass.

The earthwork mounds of the abbey itself seem to indicate the normal Cistercian arrangement for a small monastic house. The cloister garth, west and south ranges show up particularly well, with further building foundations to the south-west and south-east. South of the abbey buildings are two small escarpments leading down to a wide marshy area in the valley bottom. Here there is evidence of a complex water-control system which cannot entirely be explained by fieldwork, whereas to the east of the site of the abbey church there are clear remains of small water channels and a series of small fish-breeding stews.

Field b, to the north of the abbey buildings, has a large bank around it, in some places retaining a ditch on its outer side. Along the north side of this field the bank acts as a levee along the River Arrow, and midway across this side there is a channel leading off through the bank to the large fishponds in the next field. It seems that this large bank represents the early precinct boundary of the abbey, and, at least on the north side, it acts also as a flood barrier against the river.

Field c, to the north-east of the abbey, contains three large fishponds supplied by the leat described above and discharging into a stream flowing along the south boundary of the abbey complex. South of the fishponds lies a further mesh of small water channels (associated with the small ponds by the abbey) and what appear to be former meanders of the River Arrow. To the north, between the large fishponds and the river, there are series of banks and channels which in the west are parallel to the river but which farther east diverge across the field to where there is a complex of small streams. At the moment these features seem to indicate a smaller, later precinct boundary bank in association with a leat alongside the Arrow.

Field d, south of *Field c*, is a small triangular enclosure which must have formed part of the abbey field before the straight leat of the Forge Mill was constructed (possibly in the eighteenth century). This field contains the remains of a small fishpond which has been cut obliquely by the leat. However, the west end can still be seen in the south-east corner of the field containing the abbey.

Field e, which lies south-east of the fishponds, has an intricate complex of earthworks. In the northern half the smaller precinct boundary continues over the stream from the last section south-eastwards and into the field immediately to the east. The southern part of the field is laced with small water channels running from the old stream via gaps in the bank along the stream-side, to be collected and discharged to the north-east. These appear to have been either drainage or irrigation channels associated with some as yet unknown agricultural enterprise. The southern boundary of the field is marked by a small escarpment cut into by post-medieval sandpits.

Field f, the last, most easterly field, contains on its eastern margin an industrial site. The main earthwork feature is a large triangular pond marked by an impressive surrounding bank. To the north is a further complex of drainage channels, and to the east an array of hollows and platforms, some of which seem to be associated with the triangular pond.

Interpretation of the earthworks
Although explanations of these earthworks without excavation can be of dubious value, there does appear to be a definite sequence in their construction. It seems that the site of the abbey was originally surrounded by a large precinct bank, within which was formed the main building complex and a small series of fishponds down beside

the small stream. Outside the precinct, at least on the east and south sides, the valley was wide and marshy.

At some time, probably fairly early in the history of the abbey, an ambitious drainage and land-reclamation scheme was initiated, involving the movement of the course of the river to the north on a more or less straight course along the valley side. After the area had been drained, a series of linear fishponds was set out along the lower parts of the valley, with attendant leats and overflow channels. A field of drainage or irrigation channels was constructed south-east of these. Industrial activity was established well away from the abbey in this phase of development, and it may be that the large triangular pond was built, across and partly obliterating the boundary bank in this area, to provide water power for this industry. North-east of this large drained area the Cistercian monks could not deal with the very marshy and waterlogged condition of the ground, and the boundary bank on the north and north-east sides appears to reflect the limit of their reclamation.

PUBLICATION

We shall now conclude with a discussion on a very important aspect of fieldwork – the publication of results. Unpublished or unavailable fieldwork makes little contribution to the understanding of a site or an area. A considerable amount of fieldwork is carried out each year, much of it uncoordinated, as part of work for projects, dissertations and theses in schools and colleges, but its findings are rarely disseminated. It is poor training for students to be taught how to collect information but not how to make sure that other people learn of its existence. All landscape fieldwork, however modest, should be made available in some form to other workers. At the very least it should be reported in local archaeological or historical newsletters, notes and news sections in archaeological journals, or copies should be lent to the local museum or library for copying. Ideally, copies of work should be sent to the Directorate of Ancient Monuments and Historic Buildings, the Ordnance Survey Archaeology Division, and the National Monuments Record as the main repositories of historical landscape information.[7] More significant surveys of fully recorded sites should be published in local or national journals in the same way as excavation reports. Even plans meant for theses or projects can be copied and published, or placed in accessible public repositories. A county or regional Sites and Monuments Record should certainly receive a copy of all local work.

If possible, the information on the basic record maps should be made available to local planning authorities, as well as to the archaeologically interested bodies named above. The fieldworker should make contact with the relevant authority and offer to transcribe the information on to its maps, where all the scheduled sites should already be marked. It is probably best to choose the most important known or suspected sites, although all the information can be made available in an alternative form. It is unlikely that the authorities would, for instance, be interested in the provenance of every single sherd of medieval pottery. It is important, none the less, that such information should be available since increasingly the planning process is taking into consideration historical and archaeological information when making decisions about redevelopment projects. British legislation concerning ancient monuments is lamentably poor, particularly when compared with that of some of our continental neighbours, but the situation can be improved by the spread of information concerning known sites and the probable location of others. The archaeological education of those people who make decisions about, and are responsible for, our environment is a matter of prime importance. Too often irrevocable decisions are made apparently in ignorance of the archaeological and historical implications.

Notes and references to this chapter begin on p 192

Notes and References

ABBREVIATIONS

Ag Hist Rev	Agricultural History Review
Ant J	Antiquaries Journal
Arch J	The Archaeological Journal
Arch Rev	Archaeological Review
BAJ	Bedfordshire Archaeological Journal
Bod Lib	Bodleian Library, Oxford
CBA	Council for British Archaeology
Geog J	Geographical Journal
HMSO	Her Majesty's Stationery Office
JBAA	The Journal of the British Archaeological Association
Med Arch	Medieval Archaeology
OHS	Oxford Historical Society
TBAS	Transactions of the Birmingham Archaeological Society
TIBG	Transactions of the Institute of British Geographers
TLAHS	Transactions of the Leicestershire Archaeological and Historical Society
TSAS	Transactions of the Shropshire Archaeological Society
TWAS	Transactions of the Worcestershire Archaeological Society

INTRODUCTION

1 Rowley, R. T. and Davies, M. E. (eds). *Archaeology and the M.40 Motorway* (1973); Fowler, P. J. and Waltheu, C. V. (eds). 'Archaeology and the M.5 Motorway', *Trans of the Bristol and Gloucs Arch Soc*, Vol 90 (1971); Fowler, P. J. (ed). 'M.5 and Archaeology', *Arch Rev*, no 6 (1971)

CHAPTER I

1. Higgitt, J. C. 'The Roman Background to Medieval England', *JBAA*, 36, 3rd Series (1973)
2. Hassall, T. G. 'Excavations at Oxford', *Oxoniensia*, 36 (1971); see also Harvey, J. H. (ed). *William Worcester's Itineraries* (1969)
3. Bod Lib, MS Top Gen, C 25
4. Rickman, J. (ed). *Life of Thomas Telford* (1838)
5. Fowler, P. J. (ed). *Archaeology and the Landscape, Essays for L. V. Grinsell* (1972)
6. Prof J. K. S. St Joseph also collaborated with Dr D. Knowles to produce a similar work covering monasteries, *Monastic Sites From the Air* (1952)
7. Hoskins, W. G. *The Making of the English Landscape* (1955); Balchin, W. G. C. *Cornwall* (1955); Millward, R. *Lancashire* (1955); Finberg, H. P. R. *Gloucestershire* (1955); Hoskins, W. G. *Leicestershire* (1955) Raistrick, A. *The West Riding of Yorkshire* (1970); Taylor, C. *Dorset* (1970); Rowley, R. T. *The Shropshire Landscape* (1972); Scarfe, N. *The Suffolk Landscape* (1972); Newton, R. *The Northumberland Landscape* (1972); Emery, F. V. *The Oxfordshire Landscape* (1974)
8. Fowler, E. (ed). *Field Survey in British Archaeology* (1972)
9. Published by Shire Publications, titles to date include *Abbeys and Priories*; *Castles*; *Windmills*; *Archaeology* and a number of county archaeology books
10. Hoskins, W. G. 'The Rebuilding of Rural England, 1570-1640', *Provincial England* (1965)
11. For example, Rahtz, P. A. et al. *Medieval Sites in the Mendip, Cotswold, Wye Valley and Bristol Region*, Bristol Archaeological Research Group, Field Guide No 3 (1969)
12. Taylor, C. 'Total Archaeology', in Rogers, A. and Rowley, R. T. (eds). *Documents and Landscapes* (1974)
13. 'Rescue', the trust for British archaeology, was established in 1970 to drawn public attention to this problem. Its address is 25 The Tything, Worcester. See also 'Field Archaeology in The Future: The Crisis and the Challenge', in Fowler, P. (ed). *Archaeology and the Landscape* (1972); and Thomas, C. A. 'Ethics in archaeology 1971', *Antiquity*, Vol 45 (1971)
14. Aston, M. 'The Earthworks of Bordesley Abbey, Redditch, Worcestershire', *Med Arch*, XVI (1972), 133

Notes and References

CHAPTER 2

1. The Soil Survey of England and Wales, Rothamsted Experimental Station, Harpenden, Herts
2. Trueman, A. E. *The Scenery of England and Wales* (1938), and Stamp, D. *Britain's Structure and Scenery* (1949), provide excellent introductory books to this topic
3. Benson, D. and Fasham, P. 'Fieldwork at Chastleton', *Oxoniensia*, 37 (1972)
4. Aston, M. A. *Stonesfield Slate* (1974)
5. Brunskill, R. W. *Illustrated Handbook of Vernacular Architecture* (1970); Clifton-Taylor, A. *The Pattern of English Building*, new ed (1972)
6. Arkell, W. J. *Oxford Stone* (1947); Purcell, D. *Cambridge Stone* (1967)
7. British Museum Handbook. *Flint Implements*, 3rd ed (1968); and Oakley, K. P. *Man the Toolmaker*, 5th ed (1961)
8. Eames, E. S. *Medieval Tiles* (British Museum 1968)
9. See Fryer, D. H. *Surveying for the Archaeologist*, 4th ed (1971); Coles, J. *Field Archaeology in Britain* (1972), Ch 3; and Atkinson, R. J. C. *Field Archaeology*, 2nd ed (1953), 85–138
10. The Director General, Ordnance Survey, Romsey Road, Maybush, Southampton, SO9 4DH
11. Beresford, M. W. and Hurst, J. G. *Deserted Medieval Villages* (1971), 120
12. Biddle, M., 'The Deserted Medieval Village of Seacourt, Berks', *Oxoniensia*, Vols 26–7 (1961–2)
13. Fox, C., O'Neal, B. H. St J. and Grimes, W. F. 'Linear Earthworks Methods of Study', *Ant J* (1946), 175–9. See also Fox, A. and C. 'Wansdyke Reconsidered', *Arch J*, 115 (1960)
14. Good studies include Margary, I. D. *Roman Ways in the Weald* (1948) and *Roman Roads in Britain* (1967); and The Viatores. *Roman Roads in the South-East Midlands* (1964)
15. Brunskill, R. W. *Illustrated Handbook of Vernacular Architecture* (1971); a classic regional study is Wood-Jones, R. B. *Traditional Domestic Architecture of the Banbury Region* (1963). The Vernacular Architecture Group publishes a journal, *Vernacular Architecture*. Information about the Group can be obtained from its Secretary, Commander E. H. D. Williams, Keepers Cottage, Lower Ham, Langport, Somerset
16. The Secretary, English Place-Name Society, University College of London, Gower Street, London, WC1
17. Among the most valuable are Piggot, S. 'Archaeological Draughtsmanship, 1', *Antiquity*, Vol XXXIX (Sept 1965); Hope-Taylor, B.

'Archaeological Draughtsmanship, 2', *Antiquity*, Vol XL (June 1966); Hope-Taylor, B. 'Archaeological Draughtsmanship, 3', *Antiquity*, Vol XLI (Sep 1967); Hodgkiss, A. G. *Maps for Books and Theses* (1970); Monkhouse, F. J. and Wilkinson, H. R. *Maps and Diagrams*, 3rd imp (1966)

CHAPTER 3

1 Apart from the various county journal indexes, useful starting points are provided by Gomme, G. L. (ed). *The Index of Archaeological Papers 1665-1890* (1907); *Index of Archaeological Papers*, published annually between 1891 and 1900, and *A Guide to the Historical and Archaeological Publications of Societies in England and Wales, 1901-1933*, compiled by Mullins, E. L. C. (1968). Since 1940 the Council for British Archaeology has published an annual *Archaeological Bibliography for Great Britain and Ireland*. The early volumes are called the *Archaeological Bulletin*
2 A few of the most important books on the subject are Hoskins, W. G. *Local History in England* (1959); Kuhlicke, F. W. and Emmison, F. C. (eds). *English Local History Handlist* (1965) (for printed material); Emmison, F. L. *Archives and Local History* (1966); West, J. *Village Records* (1962); Pugh, R. B. *How to Write a Parish History*, 6th ed (1954); and Tait, J. *The Parish Chest*, new ed (1960); but there are a number of papers on different types of document, many of them to be found in the quarterly journal the *Local Historian*, published by the Standing Conference for Local History, the National Council of Social Service, 26 Bedford Square, London, WC1B 3HV
3 Colvin, H. M. (ed). *The History of the King's Works*, Vol 1 (1963)
4 Hollings, M. (ed). 'The Red Book of Worcester', Parts I–IV, *Worcestershire Historical Society* (1934-50)
5 Aston, M. 'Earthworks at the Bishop's Palace, Alvechurch, Worcestershire', *TWAS*, 3rd series, Vol 3 (1970-72)
6 Salzman, L. F. *Building in England down to 1540* (1952), 536
7 See, for instance, *Maps and Plans in the Public Record Office, 1, British Isles, 1410-1860* (1967)
8 For example, Harvey, P. D. A. and Thorpe, H. *The Printed Maps of Warwickshire, 1576-1900* (1959)
9 Harley, J. B. *Maps for the Local Historian. A Guide to the British Sources* (1972)
10 See, for example, *Maps of Cheshire, 1577-1900* (1942) and *A Gloucestershire and Bristol Atlas*, The Bristol and Gloucestershire Archaeological Society (1961)

Notes and References

11 First-class examples of this technique can be seen in V. Skipp's *Discovering Sheldon* (1960), *Discovering Bickenhill* (1963) and *Medieval Yardley* (1970)
12 Salop County Record Office, 112 uncat. See also Chaplin, R. 'Discovering Lost Ironworks', *The Local Historian*, Vol 9, No 2 (1970)
13 Oxfordshire County Record Office IV/3. Rowley, R. T. 'First Report on Excavations at Middleton Stoney 1970-71', *Oxoniensia*, 37 (1973)
14 Prince, H. *Parks in England* (1967)
15 Society for the Preservation of Ancient Buildings, the Wind and Water Mills Section.
   1 Wilson, P. N. *Watermills – An Introduction*
   2 Wailes, R. *Tide Mills Part I*
   3 Wailes, R. *Tide Mills Part II*
   4 Wailes, R. *Tide Mills Part III*; Gardener, E. M. *The Three Mills, Bromley-by-Bow*
   5 Pelham, R. A. *Fulling Mills*
   6 Reid, K. L. *The Three Mills and the Landscape*
   7 Wilson, P. N. *Watermills with Horizontal Wheels* (1960)
   8 Luckhurst, D. *Monastic Water Mills*
   9 Shorter, A. H. *Water Paper Mills in England* (1966)
16 Field, J. *Field Names* (1972). See also recent volumes of the English Place-Name Society for Gloucestershire (1965) and Cheshire (1972)
17 Reproduced in Salter, H. E. and Cooke, A. H. (eds). 'Boarstall Cartulary', *OHS*, LXXXVIII (1930)
18 Beresford, M. W. 'Fallowfield, Northumberland: An Early Cartographic Representation of a Deserted Village', *Med Arch*, Vol 10
19 Emmison, F. C. *Archives and Local History* (1966)
20 Mr Tate produced an index map 'A Domesday of English Enclosure Acts and Awards', *The Amateur Historian*, Vol 5 (1963). Many County Record Offices have prepared easily digestible lists of their enclosure documents
21 The location of tithe maps is an easier task. *The Return of all Tithes Commuted and Apportioned under the Acts for Commutation of Tithes* (British Sessional Papers, House of Commons, 1887, Vol LXIV, 239-533), is effectively a complete list of all districts (parish, townships, or smaller unit) for which tithe apportionments exist
22 Public Records Office, Chancery Lane, London, EC1. The tithe documents are stored at Ashridge, Berkhamsted, Hertfordshire
23 See also Close, Sir C. *The Early Years of the Ordnance Survey*, new ed (1969)
24 David & Charles have republished a large number of the first edition of the OS 1in maps

CHAPTER 4

1 We are indebted to J. Hampton, J. Pickering and D. Riley for advice on this chapter
2 Crawford, O. G. S. *Air Survey and Archaeology* (1924), *Wessex from the Air* (1928), *Air Photography for Archaeologists* (1929), *Luftbild und Vorgeschichte* (1938)
3 Cropmarks had been recognised from the ground in the Upper Thames Valley by antiquarians during the nineteenth century, notably John Stone at Standlake and F. Haverfield at Long Wittenham, and air photographs of cropmarks of the Big Rings Henge at Dorchester-on-Thames were taken as early as 1922-3
4 A painstaking contour plan of the ridge and furrow at Hen Domen (Mont) revealed that the eleventh-century motte and bailey castle lay on top of traces of pre-Norman cultivation. Barker, P. A. and Lawson, J. 'A Pre-Norman field system at Hen Domen', *Med Arch*, XV (1971), 58
5 A general plan of the distribution of ridge and furrow in the south Midlands has been compiled from aerial photographs, *Geog J*, 131 (3) (1965), 366-9
6 Williams, R. B. G. 'Frost and the works of Man', *Antiquity*, XLVII (1973)
7 Webster, G. and Hobley, B. 'Aerial Reconnaissance over the Warwickshire Avon', *Arch J*, CXXI (1964); Baker, A. 'Aerial Reconnaissance over Viroconium and Military Sites in the Area in 1969', *TSAS*, 59 (1969-70); Hollowell, R. 'Aerial Photography and Fieldwork in the Upper Nene Valley', *Bull of the Northamptonshire Fed of Arch Societies*, No 6 (September 1971); Benson, D. and Miles, D. *The Upper Thames Valley - An Archaeological Survey of the River Gravels* (1974)
8 Colvin, H. (ed). *The History of the King's Works*, Vol 1 (1963)
9 Rahtz, P. A. 'A Possible Saxon Palace near Stratford-upon-Avon', *Antiquity*, XLIV (June 1970)
10 Addyman, P. V., Leigh, D. and Hughes, M. J. 'Anglo-Saxon Houses at Chalton, Hampshire', *Med Arch*, 16 (1973)
11 Riley, D. N. 'The Technique of Air Archaeology', *Arch J*, CI (1944)
12 The address of the National Monuments Record is Fortress House, Savile Row, London, W1X 2AA. The collection of archaeological photographs includes the work of J. Pickering, mainly in north Northamptonshire, Leicestershire, Trent Valley, Welland Valley and the Upper Warwickshire Avon, and the Cherwell and Thames in Oxfordshire; A. Baker in the Avon-Severn Valleys and the Upper

Thames; and D. Riley in north Lincolnshire, the north Trent Valley and the area north of Doncaster, where a large new area of cropmarks has recently been recognised

13 *Peterborough New Town – A Survey of Antiquities in the Area of Development* (1969)
14 Romsey Road, Maybush, Southampton SO9 4DH
15 11 West Road, Cambridge, CB3 9DP
16 BKS Surveys Ltd, Cleeve Road, Leatherhead, Surrey; Fairey Surveys Ltd, Reform Road, Maidenhead, Berkshire; Meridian Airmaps Ltd, Commerce Way, Lancing, Sussex; Aerofilms Ltd, 4 Albemarle Street, London, W1; Hunting Survey Ltd, 6 Elstree Road, Boreham Wood, Herts

CHAPTER 5

1 See, for instance, Lobel, M. D. (ed). *Historic Towns Atlas*, Vol 1 (1969), which includes Banbury, Caernarvon, Glasgow, Gloucester, Hereford, Nottingham, Reading and Salisbury. Eventually it is hoped to cover many of the major provincial towns in Britain
2 Heighway, C. M. *The Erosion of History* (1972). This survey also contains special case studies of Abingdon (Berks), Cambridge, Gloucester, Kingston upon Hull (Yorks), Ruthin (Denbighshire) and Stirling
3 HMSO (1963)
4 CBA Memorandum on the Implications of the Buchanan Report (1964)
5 Such as Benson, D. and Cook, J. *City of Oxford Redevelopment Archaeological Implications* (1967); Tamworth Research Committee. *Tamworth Development – The Archaeological Implications* (1971); Miles, D. and Fowler, P. J. *Tewkesbury – The Archaeological Implications of Development* (1972); Addyman, P. V. and Rumsby, J. H. *The Archaeological Implications of Proposed Development in York* (1972); Simpson, C. *Wallingford – The Archaeological Implications of Redevelopment* (1973); and Biddle, M. (ed). *The Future of London's Past* (1973)
6 See Beresford, M. W. *New Towns of the Middle Ages*, Ch 2 (1967), and Benton, J. F. (ed). *Town Origins, The Evidence from Medieval England* (1968)
7 Carter, H. *The Towns of Wales* (1966) cites the examples of Caernarvon, Aberystwyth, Cardigan and Cardiff, where the present commercial centre is different from the medieval centre
8 Rowley, R. T. *The Shropshire Landscape* (1972) and Renn, D. *Norman Castles in Britain* (1968)

Notes and References

9 Beresford, M. W. *New Towns of the Middle Ages* (1967), 188
10 A good example of the development of a nineteenth-century town is provided by Riley, R. C. *The Growth of Southsea as a Naval Satellite and Victorian Resort*, The Portsmouth Papers, No 16 (1972)
11 The planned element in Scottish medieval towns appears to be just as strong as in the towns of England and Wales; see Simpson, G. C. (ed). *Scotland's Medieval Burghs* (1972)
12 *VCH Warks*, Vol III (1945), 31
13 *VCH Oxon*, Vol III (1962), 163
14 Salter, H. E. 'Oxford City Properties', *OHS*, LXXXIII (1926), *Map of Medieval Oxford* (1934), and 'Survey of Oxford, I & II', *OHS*, new series, Vol 14 (1960) and Vol 20 (1969), ed by Pantin, W. A.; Urry, W. *Canterbury under the Angevin Kings* (1967)
15 Smith, T. P. 'The Medieval Town Defences of King's Lynn', *JBAA*, 3rd vol, 33 (1970); O'Neil, B. H. St J. 'Southampton Town Wall', in Grimes, W. F. (ed). *Aspects of Archaeology in Britain and Beyond* (1951); Turner, H. L. *Town Defences in England and Wales* (1970); Harvey, A. *The Castles and Walled Towns of England* (1911)
16 However, much can be learned from Smith, J. T. and Yates, E. M. 'Dating of English Houses from External Evidence', *Field Studies*, Vol 2, No 5 (1968), 202
17 Pantin, W. A. 'Medieval English Town House Plans', *Med Arch*, VI–VII (1962–3), and 'Some Medieval English Town Houses', in Foster, I. L. and Alcock, L. (eds). *Culture and Environment* (1963)
18 Hudson, K. *Handbook for Industrial Archaeologists* (1967) and *Industrial Archaeology* (1963); Buchanan, R. A. *The Theory and Practice of Industrial Archaeology* (1968); Pannell, J. P. M. *Techniques of Industrial Archaeology* (1966). David & Charles also publish a series of regional industrial archaeology studies
19 Beresford, M. W. *New Towns of the Middle Ages* (1967), 525
20 Hutton, K. 'Streets called "Gate"', *Local Historian*, Vol 8, No 8 (1969), 288

CHAPTER 6

1 An interesting attempt has recently been made by Prof B. Cunliffe to explain the siting of villages in Hampshire in 'Saxon and Medieval Settlement Patterns in the Region of Chalton, Hampshire', *Med Arch*, XVI (1973)
2 Renn, D. *Norman Castles in Britain* (1968)
3 See, for example, Conzen, M. R. G. 'Alnwick, Northumberland', *TIBG*, No 27 (1960)

4   Hawkes, S. C. and Gray, M. 'Preliminary Note on the Early Anglo-Saxon Settlement at New Wintles Farm, Eynsham', *Oxoniensia*, 34 (1969)
5   Roberts, B. K. 'Village Plans', *Local Historian*, Vol 9, No 5 (1971), and 'Village Plans in County Durham: A Preliminary Statement', *Med Arch*, XVI (1973)
6   Batey, M. 'Nuneham Courtenay: An Oxfordshire 18th Century Deserted Village', *Oxoniensia*, 38 (1968).
7   Anderson, M. D. *History and Imagery in British Churches* (1971)
8   Thomas, C. *The Early Christian Archaeology of North Britain* (1971)
9   House, V. M. *Pusey – A Village Record* (1972), 46, gives two maps of extensions in 1880 and 1911 to this Berkshire churchyard
10 Jesson, Margaret. *The Archaeology of Churches* (CBA 1973)
11 See Eden, P. 'Studying your Parish Church from the Building', *Amateur Historian*, Vol 7, No 2 (1962)
12 Taylor, H. M. and Joan. *Anglo-Saxon Architecture* (1965)
13 Thorpe, H. 'The Green Villages of County Durham', *TIBG*, No 15 (1951), 49, and 'The Green Villages as a Distinctive Form of Settlement on the North European Plain', *Bull de la Soc Belge d'Etudes Geogr*, 30 (1961)
14 Bond, C. J. 'The Estates of Evesham Abbey: A Preliminary Survey of Their Medieval Topography', *Vale of Evesham Historical Society Research Papers*, Vol IV (1973)
15 Cook, A. O. *A Book of Dovecotes* (1920)
16 See, for example, Wood-Jones, R. B. *Traditional Domestic Architecture in the Banbury Region* (1963)

CHAPTER 7

1   See, for example, Skipp, V. *Discovering Sheldon* (1960) and *Discovering Bickenhill* (1963)
2   Skipp, V. *Medieval Yardley* (1970)
3   Beresford, M. W. *The Lost Villages of England* (1954); Beresford, M. W. and Hurst J. G. *Deserted Medieval Villages* (1971). The latter contains a comprehensive bibliography, together with a gazetteer of all known sites. A useful general introduction to the subject is provided by Allison, K. *Deserted Villages* (1970). The Secretary of the Group is J. G. Hurst, 67 Gloucester Crescent, London, NW1, who would be pleased to hear of new sites or receive surveys or records of known sites.
4   A photograph of the site in its undisturbed state appears in St Joseph, J. K. S. (ed). *The Uses of Air Photography* (1966)

Notes and References

5 Beresford, M. W. 'A Journey among Deserted Villages', *History on the Ground* (1957)
6 At Detton, Salop, an apparently good DMV proved upon excavation to have been ground severely disturbed by marling. Stanford, S. *TSAS*, 58 (1967)
7 A good example of this approach is Hall, D. W. 'Modern Surveys of Medieval Field Systems', *BAJ*, Vol 7 (1972)
8 Pigott, C. D. 'Nettles as Indicators of Soil Conditions', *New Scientist*, Vol 21, 230–2
9 Allison, K. J., Beresford, M. W. and Hurst J. G. *The Deserted Villages of Northamptonshire* (1966)
10 Robinson, M. 'Excavation at Tetsworth', *Oxoniensia*, 38 (1974)
11 Bowen, H. C. *Ancient Fields* (1961); Orwin, C. S. and Orwin, C. S. *The Open Fields*, 3rd ed (1967). A good summary of all recent work on the origin of the open fields is contained in Finberg, H. P. R. (ed). *The Agrarian History of England and Wales*, Vol 1, Part 2, AD 43–1042 (1972)
12 Beckwith, I. 'The Remodelling of a Common-field System', *Ag Hist Rev*, XV (1967)
13 See Beresford and St Joseph (1958). *Medieval England: An Aerial Survey* and Mead, W. R. 'Ridge and Furrow in Bucks', *Geog J*, CXX (1954)
14 It should be remembered, however, that 'castle' is used indiscriminately to describe earthwork sites, including, for example, the massive hillfort of Maiden Castle, Dorset
15 See also Renn, D. *Norman Castles in Britain* (1968)
16 Thompson, M. W. 'Reclamation of Waste Ground for the Pleasance at Kenilworth Castle, Warwickshire', *Med Arch*, VIII (1964), 222–3, and 'Two Levels of the Mere at Kenilworth Castle, Warwickshire', *Med Arch*, IX (1965), 156; Drew, J. H. 'Notes on the Water System at Kenilworth Castle', *TBAS*, 81 (1966), and 'Kenilworth Castle – A Discussion of Its Entrances', *TBAS*, 84 (1971)
17 C. Taylor has suggested that the moats in Cambridgeshire at least were not intended to perform any defensive function, in 'Medieval Moats in Cambridgeshire', *Archaeology and the Landscape* (1972), 237
18 For typical forms see Emery, F. V. 'Moated Settlements in England', *Geography*, XLVII, Part 4 (1962); Roberts, B. K. 'Moated Sites', *Amateur Historian*, 34 (1962)
19 An interesting example of this at Bottisham Park (Cambridgeshire) is cited by Taylor, C., in 'Maps, Documents and Fieldwork', *Field Survey in British Archaeology* (CBA 1972)

Notes and References

20 The Secretary is F. A. Aberg, 'Elmsett', Forest Lane, Kirklevington, York
21 Beresford and St Joseph. *Medieval England: An Aerial Survey* (1958) 64
22 See also Roberts, B. K. 'Medieval Fishponds', *Amateur Historian*, 7, No 4 (1966), and Allcroft, A. H. *Earthwork of England* (1908), 467, 477, 489-92
23 Aston, M. A. *Med Arch*, Vol XVI (1972)
24 Crawford, O. G. S. *Archaeology in the Field* (1953). See also Cantor, L. M. 'The Medieval Parks of Leicestershire', *TLAHS*, XLVI (1970-71)
25 Finberg, H. P. R. *The Early Charters of Devon and Cornwall* (1953), *The Early Charters of the West Midlands* (1961), and *The Early Charters of Wessex* (1966)
26 For an introduction to monastic granges see Platt, C. *The Monastic Grange in Medieval England* (1969)
27 Information from P. A. Rahtz
28 For a guide to the extensive literature on enclosures see Brewer, J. G. *Enclosures and the Open Field, a Bibliography* (1972)
29 *Hedges and Local History*, published for the standing conference for Local History by the National Council for Social Service (1971). An example of the application of the hedge-dating technique is explained in Hewlett, C. 'Reconstructing a Historical Landscape from Field and Documentary Evidence: Otford in Kent', *Ag Hist Rev*, Vol 21 (1973)
30 See, for example, Money, J. H. 'Medieval Iron Workings in Minepit Wood, Rotherfield, Sussex', *Med Arch*, XV (1971); and Chaplin, R. 'Discovering Lost Ironworks', *The Local Historian*, Vol 9, 2 (1970)
31 Lineham, Catherine. 'Deserted Sites and Rabbit Warrens on Dartmoor, Devon', *Med Arch*, X (1966)

CHAPTER 8

1 Benson, D. 'A Sites and Monuments Record for the Oxford Region', *Oxoniensia*, 37 (1973)
2 For some brief comments on the problems of cataloguing see Renfrew, C. 'The Requirements of the Research Worker in Archaeology', *Museums Journal*, 67 (2) (1967)
3 Benson, D. and Miles, D. *The Upper Thames Valley: An Archaeological Survey of the River Gravels* (1974)
4 Cf Hislop, R. 'Information Retrieval and Computer Printed Indexes', *Museums Journal*, 67 (2) (1967) – a paper given at a Colloquium on Information Retrieval for Museums, Sheffield, 1967

5 Sheppard, P. 'A County Society: the Cornwall Checklists', in *Field Survey in British Archaeology* (1972); and Thomas, C. 'The Present Significance of Fieldwork in the Light of the Cornish Parochial Check-list Survey', *Archaeology and the Landscape* (1972)
6 All the excavation reports are published in *Oxoniensia*, 38 (1974)
7 Directorate of Ancient Monuments and Historic Buildings, Department of the Environment, Fortress House, 23 Savile Row, London, W1X 2AA. The National Monuments Record is at the same address

Appendices

1 *Victoria County History published volumes up to July 1973*

General Introduction
Bedfordshire, Vols I, II, III, Index (complete)
Berkshire, Vols I, II, III, IV, Index (complete
Buckinghamshire, Vols I, II, III, IV, Index (complete)
Cambridgeshire, Vols I, II, III, IV, Index to volumes I–IV
Cornwall, Vols I, II
Cumberland, Vols I, II
Derbyshire, Vols I, II
Devon, Vol I
Dorset, Vols II, III
Durham, Vols I, II, III
Essex, Vols I, II, III, IV, V, Bibliography
Gloucestershire, Vols II, VI, VIII, X
Hampshire, Vols I, II, III, IV, V, Index (complete)
Herefordshire, Vol I
Hertfordshire, Vols, I, II, III, IV, Index (complete)
Huntingdonshire, Vols I, II, III, Index (complete)
Kent, Vols I, II, III
Lancashire, Vols I, II, III, IV, V, VI, VII, VIII (complete)
Leicestershire, Vols I, II, III, IV, V
Lincolnshire, Vol II
London, Vol I
Middlesex, Vols, I, II, III, IV
Norfolk, Vols, I, II
Northamptonshire, Vols, I, II, III, IV
Nottinghamshire, Vols I, II
Oxfordshire, Vols I, II, III, V, VI, VII, VIII, IX, X
Rutland, Vols, I, II, Index (complete)

Shropshire, Vols I, II, VIII
Somerset, Vols I, II
Staffordshire, Vols, I, II, III, IV, V, VIII
Suffolk, Vols I, II
Surrey, Vols I, II, III, IV, Index (complete)
Sussex, Vols I, II, III, IV, VII, IX
Warwickshire, Vols I, II, III, IV, V, VI, VII, VIII, Index to volumes I–VI (complete). Stratford-upon-Avon (off-print)
Wiltshire, Vols I (part i), II, III, IV, V, VI, VII, VIII, IX
Worcestershire, Vols I, II, III, IV (Index (complete)
Yorkshire (general volumes), Vols I, II, III, Index (complete)
Yorkshire, East Riding, Vol I
Yorkshire, North Riding, Vols I, II, Index (complete)
Yorkshire, City of York, complete vol

2   *Royal Commission volumes on ancient and historical monuments published up to July 1973*

ENGLAND: Inventories: *Hertfordshire* (1910); *Buckinghamshire* (2 vols, 1912–13); *Essex* (4 vols, 1916–23); *London* (5 vols, 1924–30); *Huntingdonshire* (1926); *Herefordshire* (3 vols, 1931–4); *Westmorland* (1936); *Middlesex* (1937); *Oxford, City of* (1939); *Dorset* (4 vols, in seven parts, 1952–72); *Cambridge, City of* (2 vols, plus maps, 1959); *York, Roman* (1962); *City of York, Defences* (1973); *Cambridgeshire, West* (2 vols, 1968–72); *City of York, South-West* (1973).
Smaller Publications: *Guide to St. Albans Cathedral* (1952); *A Matter of Time* (1960); *Monuments Threatened or Destroyed* (1963); *Newark on Trent, Civil War Siegeworks* (1964); *Survey of Peterborough New Town* (1969); *Shielings and Castles* (1970)

SCOTLAND: Inventories: *Sutherland* (1910); *Caithness* (1911); *Galloway, Wigtownshire* (1913); *Galloway, Kirkcudbrightshire* (1914); *Berwickshire* (1909, revised 1915); *Dumfriesshire* (1920); *East Lothian* (1924); *Outer Hebrides, Skye etc* (1928); *Mid and West Lothian* (1929); *Fife, Kinross and Clackmannan* (1933); *Orkney and Shetland* (3 vols, 1946); *Edinburgh, City of* (1951); *Roxburghshire* (2 vols, 1956); *Selkirk* (1957); *Stirlingshire* (2 vols, 1963); *Peeblesshire* (2 vols, 1967)

WALES: Inventories: *Montgomeryshire* (1911); *Flintshire* (1912); *Radnorshire* (1913); *Denbighshire* (1914); *Carmarthenshire* (1917); *Merioneth* (1921); *Pembrokeshire* (1925); *Anglesey* (1937, reprinted 1970); *Caernarvonshire* (3 vols, 1956, 1960, 1964)
Smaller Publications: *County Hand-Lists of Field Monuments 1, Cardiganshire* (1970)

Appendices

3 *Brunskill building recording form and cards*

GREAT HOUSE	LARGE HOUSE	(SMALL HOUSE)	COTTAGE

LOCATION	COUNTY	MAP REFERENCE	FILING
BURGH	CUMBERLAND	NY 321 591	344
ADDRESS	ASPECT	WALLING MATERIAL	DATE
West End, Burgh-by-Sands	SSE	brick, sandstone dressings	–

WALL	ADMIX.	WINDOWS₁	WINDOWS₂	ROOF	MATERIALS	M.M.	CHIMNEYS	DORMERS	S.F.₁	S.F.₂	S.F.₃	S.F.₄
83--1	--14-			4732-	4372-	5-44-	12---	75-4-		13---		--76-

REMARKS :—

PHOTOGRAPH /OVER

SURVEYOR	DATE	PHOTOGRAPH No.
R.W.B.	April 56	SG2/28

	LARGE HOUSE	(SMALL HOUSE)	COTTAGE

LOCATION	COUNTY	ADDRESS	MAP REFERENCE	FILING
BURGH	CUMBERLAND	West End, Burgh-by-Sands	NY 321 591	344
SURVEYOR	SURVEY DATE	FILM No.	EXPOSURE No.	ELEV. PHOTO	ASPECT	WALLING MATERIAL	DATE
R.W.B.	April 56	SG 2	28		SSE	brick, sandstone dressing	—

CODED DESCRIPTION

PHOTOGRAPH

196

Appendices

		LARGE HOUSE	SMALL HOUSE		COTTAGE
parish	county		address	map ref	serial
surveyor & date	exp no	aspect		wall material	date
notes		plan		elevation	

doorway

window

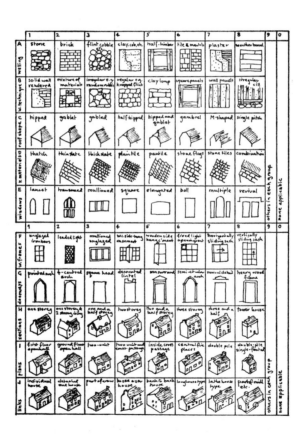

197

Appendices

4 *Medieval Village Research Group fieldwork questionnaire*

COMPLETED QUESTIONNAIRES SHOULD BE SENT TO THE SECRETARY, MEDIEVAL VILLAGE RESEARCH GROUP, 67 GLOUCESTER CRESCENT, LONDON, NW1. IF ANY QUESTION CANNOT BE ANSWERED, PLEASE STRIKE IT OUT

Completed by............................. Date..............

1. Name of county:
2. Name of site (if known):
3. Name of present parish:
4. National Grid Reference:
    (*a*) of site:
      (NB. Many of these on the MVRG lists at present relate to a modern farm while they should show the exact location of the DMV)
    (*b*) of medieval church or chapel of village (if any):
5. Name and address of owner/s:
6. Name and address of tenant/s farming the site:
7. Name and address of nearest inhabited house to the site, if not the same as (6):
8. Remarks and prospects for the future preservation of site:

THE SITE

9. At what height above sea level does the site lie, and how does this relate to the surrounding landscape?
10. On what kind of soil does the site lie and what is the geology? (You may find published geology maps helpful.)
11. If the village is on a slope, in which direction is it facing?
12. Is there a stream or spring nearby?
13. Is the site ill-drained? (If not, could this be the result of recent field drainage?)
14. Is there a well on the site, and what material is it lined with?
15. What is the relationship between the site and the church? (if any)

The Earthworks

16. Are there any earthworks, and if so, over what area do they extend? (Very often they are to be found in several adjacent fields. Mark on the first plan the fields in which earthworks of the village can be seen.)
17. Is the site sloping, terraced or all on one level?
18. Do the earthworks form a recognisable pattern or are they indistinct and vague?
19. Are the lines of the roads visible? (These usually show as sunken ways.)

Appendices

20   Can you pick out any distinct house-sites? (These are not always seen as buried wall foundations but may be represented by raised platforms, and the positions of hearths may at times be indicated by patches of nettles.)
21   Are the house platforms contained within *property enclosures*? (These are either banks, buried stone walls or ditches, depending on the geology.)
22   How do these house-sites and boundaries relate to the streets?
23   Is the village site defined by a boundary bank or ditch?
24   Are there any castle or moated sites or particularly extensive or prominent house-sites in the village, and could they represent the site(s) of the *manor house*(s)?
25   How does the site(s) of the castle or manor house(s) relate to the village?
26   Is there a village green? (This is usually a relatively level clear area in the village site, sometimes bounded by streets.)
27   Are there any ponds? (There may be a pond on the village green. It will probably have silted up too much today to contain water.)
28   Is there any evidence for post-medieval disturbance of the site, by quarrying or modern ponds, for example?
29   Are there any fishponds, millponds or mill leats nearby?

Ploughed sites
30   If the site is partly or wholly ploughed, for how long has this been done and was the site levelled first by a bulldozer?
31   Are earthworks still visible in the ploughed field?
32   Are there any signs of soil marks in the ploughsoil representing ploughed up buildings, yards and boundaries? Can you make a plan of them?
33   Are there any pieces of worked stone lying in the ploughsoil?
34   Can you collect pottery and other surface finds, bagging them by areas or fields? (If you have a 25in map record the field number. If pottery is collected by area, this should give a useful date-range for the different parts of the site and make it possible to suggest expansion and contraction within the site, if you can collect enough.)
35   If you visit the site when it is under crop, are there any signs of cropmarks?

Ridge and furrow
36   Is there any ridge and furrow visible near the village? If so, how is it related to the village?
37   Is it straight or curved?

Appendices

38 What is the width between the tops of the ridges?
39 How high are the tops of the ridges from the bottoms of the furrows?
40 If possible try to include the outline of any ridge and furrow on your plans.

PLANS

Plan 1
Show the extent and outlines of the site in the modern field system.

Plan(s) 2
Detailed plans or sketches of earthworks, etc.

STANDING BUILDINGS

41 List the standing buildings on or near the site and give if possible an approximate estimation of their date. (There may be a church, rectory, manor, farms, cottages.)
42 What are the building materials?
    (*a*) in the church
    (*b*) in other buildings
    Is it local?

The church or chape
43 Does the church occupy the highest point on the site?
44 Is the church ruined? If so, how much of it still survives?
45 If it is intact, how often is it used?
46 What is the earliest architectural style, eg Norman?
47 What is the dominant style? Does this or the size of the church indicate a period of prosperity?
48 Is there evidence of a contraction of the size of the church, eg blocked aisles?
49 To what style does the final period of alteration belong?
50 If the church is a modern building, does it contain any older features from an earlier church such as a font?
51 To what period do the interior ornaments and monuments belong?
52 What are the latest dates for the tombstones in the churchyard?
53 What shape is the churchyard and what is the churchyard boundary made of?

Other buildings of particular interest
54 Are any other buildings of particular interest or of an early date? (The best clue to the age of a house is the roof timbering.)

Appendices

DOCUMENTATION
55 Do you know of any documents mentioning the site?
56 Name and address of compiler

5   Moated Sites Research Group introduction to field card

The field card provides space for a brief comprehensive description and sketch plan of each site, and it is not intended to serve as a complete record of the varied archaeological and historical information available. The increasing rate of destruction of moated sites means that a rapid but accurate survey is needed of the field evidence, and the field card provides a guide and classification for this. Additional evidence is filed separately and photostats of maps, large-scale plans, excavation reports, notes on documentary evidence, etc will be included in these files if forwarded.

For the purposes of definition a moated site must have a ditch at least 15ft (approx 4·50m) wide. The ditch may or may not be banked, is not always flooded, and may not complete the enclosure. Sites vary greatly in manorial status but the survey may include defended manor houses and granges. Castles of the medieval period are excluded from the survey, though sites in this category can be noted when it can be demonstrated that the term 'castle' is a later title, and the site started life as a moated manor.

Appendices

1		2	3
MOATED SITES RESEARCH GROUP		J. COBBLE	13.12.72
4 YORKSHIRE, S. RIDING	5 DISHTHWAITE	6 THE MOATS	7 TA 859596
8 S. Sloping ridge 325′ OD	9 Gravel	10 N. from Church	11 1½ acres
12 Other	13 C 18th Cottage Occupied	14 On N side 15ft wide Causeway	15 2–4 ft deep Surface
16 None	17 C 15th–17th Pottery Ridge Tile	18	19 1760 Estate Map 1″. 99 6″. 94 SE
20 Single 400 × 200 ft		21 Rectangular	
22 15 ft wide × 5 ft high Internal		23 Flat	
24 30 ft 8 ft maximum		25 Wet/Revetment? Scattered stones along moat	
26 Pasture		27 Fishpond on S. Enclosure on W. 200 × 150 ft Fishponds/Banked Enclosures	
28 Both Ridges average 28–30 ft wide		29	
30 Local unnamed amateur circa 1930. Finds unrecorded			

The above card has been completed for a hypothetical site.

Appendices

1. A diagonal stroke in the top right corner on the card is used to signify that the site is scheduled.
2. Name of recorder.
3. Date of the field survey (when the site was visited).
4. County.   5 Parish.
6. Site Name.   7 National Grid Reference.
8. Topography. The physical characteristics of the site and the height above sea level: flat, slope, valley, ridge, etc.
9. Soil. Some indication of texture is required.
10. Location. This refers to human settlement, ie the village, parish boundary, church, etc.
11. Area. The area of the island or islands is required.
12. Manorial status or other, such as grange.
13. Buildings. An approximate date should be given, if possible, for the earliest building on the site or of any building adjacent.
14. Entrance. Its position should be noted, if visible, and its width. Some sites may have more than one.
15. Water Supply. This refers specifically to the moat which may have a spring or stream diverted to fill it.
16. A mill site may sometimes be related to the moat complex.
17. Surface Finds. The presence of pottery, stone, roof tile, etc should be noted.
18. Aerial Photographs. Number and location if known.
19. Maps. The numbers of OS maps and details of estate maps should be noted.
20. Enclosure Plan. Cross out whichever heading does not apply and give brief dimensions. Incomplete moats should be noted under this heading as an additional category.

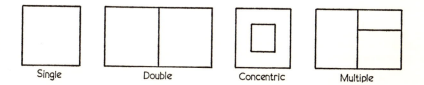

21. Enclosure Type. Cross out whichever heading is inapplicable. The sketch plan is of particular importance in amplifying the information on enclosure plan and type.
22. Enclosure Banks. Cross out whichever heading is not applicable and give brief dimensions of the width and height of the banks of the moat.

Appendices

23 Enclosure Height. Raised applies to moats possessing an internal platform above the height of the adjoining field or enclosures.
24 Moat. Dimensions of the moat to the main platform ie inhabited area. If possible give the maximum width, minimum width and depth.
25 Moat. Cross out whichever heading does not apply.
26 Condition. Cross out whichever heading does not apply or add details, eg Built over.
27 Appendages. Give brief dimensions.
28 Enclosure. Indicate the presence or absence of ridge and furrow ploughing.
29 Documentary Evidence. This only allows a brief indication of the date and nature of the evidence. Details of the evidence should be noted separately and forwarded if possible.

6 Oxford City and County Museum primary record card

OXFORD CITY AND COUNTY MUSEUM : FIELD DEPARTMENT : PRIMARY RECORD CARD.   No. 2455

Period MEDIEVAL	Item CASTLE	DOVECOTE CHAPEL		Form Classification EARTHWORKS
O.S. 6" SP 42 NE	25"	50"	Parish SOMERTON County OXON	Map Reference Area Centred SP 497289

Remarks:
1/ There is a tradition that the school stands on the site of the inner court of a castle. 8 Inhumation burials found in the grounds of the elementary school.

2/ Site of medieval castle of the De Greys in field NE of church - mounds and fishponds 1295 Extent mentions court, dovecote, fishponds (see PRN 5080) curtilages and gardens. Chapel in castle yard standing until 1580.

Authorities:
1/ Oxoniensia 17-18 1952-3 p.218
a/ Blomfield 'Deanery of Bicester' pt. IV p. 90, 93 and 152.

2/ V.C.H. Oxon Vol. 6 1959 p. 290
M. Aston 27/1/72

Present Location (if object):

Owner and Address:

A.P. Nos. SP 4928

Mus. Neg. Nos. 26/73/16 and 29

Appendices

7 *Archaeological record*

ESSEX COUNTY COUNCIL, PLANNING DEPT. – ARCHAEOLOGICAL RECORD.

O.S. 2½"/6" Sheet No	N.G.R. (8 or 10 figures)	Parish or Town	SITE RECORD
TL 52 N.W.	TL 54272873	Henham	FOR ECC. USE ONLY

SITE DESCRIPTION & OTHER INFORMATION. (Please include sketch with scale on reverse side of form where possible)

Moated site situated some 200 metres to the N.W. of St. Mary's church at 345' above O.D. The moat is rectangular in plan with an extended arm running southwards from the S.W. corner & forming western boundary to field known as Hall Crofts. The moat has causeway to the south-east and a bridge on the western side which was constructed in 1961 along with the house sited within moated enclosure. The digging of the house foundations & cess pit revealed the brick foundations of an earlier house. The moat is water filled and in good condition; the water supply appears to be from surface drainage which is retained by the clay subsoil. The enclosure itself is flat with no visible enclosure banks. The field to the south-east contains low earthworks possibly indicating a shrunken village. The moated hall was replaced by a hall within the deer park at Henham Lodge (P.R.O. survey 1530).

Present condition & potential threats to site: Some tipping alongside moat causeway. Site recommended to D.o.E. for scheduling.

Date 2·11·72

Bibliography R.C.H.M. Essex I p. 163.
The Land and Buildings of Henham — Joyce M. Winmill, 1970.

For ECC use only:
- Site No. 1004
- TL 5427 2873 N.G. Ref.
- 815 Parish or Town
- 3714 Generic Code
- 016 Period
- EX2221 Journal Ref.
- Journal Ref.
- 00 Threat
- Aerial Photo
- 004 Topographical Photo
- 52NW05 O.S. Card No.
- 2 Category
- 21172 Visit Date

Name & address of owner:

Name & address of tenant: None

Name & address of recorder: John Hedges, County Hall, Chelmsford, Essex.

Site No. 2004

- 1004 RECTANGULAR MOAT WITH EXTENDED ARM TO SOUTH & HOUSE
- 3004
- 4004 NONE
- 5004 JOHN HEDGES COUNTY HALL CHELMSFORD

N 205

Appendices

8 *Ordnance Survey conventions for site recording*

Conventional marking	Ex no	Significance of marking and notes on examples
Red cross		Marks the position, site, or find-spot of a small unpublished item to an accuracy of 25m
	1	Used for a new recorded antiquity
	2	Used for an item dealt with as miscellaneous information (misc inf)
Red sketch of detail		Indicates the approximately correct position and the approximate form of an unpublished antiquity of some size
	3	Used to mark an Iron Age fort
Red shading		Draws attention to a published item which might otherwise be overlooked, or confused with adjacent detail
	4	Used to distinguish a particular building
	5	Used to distinguish an item dealt with as misc inf
Red continuous line		Delineates the probable to correct route of a linear, or of a linear-like boundary, whether published or not
	6a	Used to indicate the course of a Roman road
	6b	Used for a park pale
Red pecked line		Marks the possible route of a linear, or of a linear-like boundary, whether published or not
	7a	Used for a Roman road
	7b	Used for a park pale
Yellow cross		Marks the position of an item which cannot be located to within 25m, but is probably correct to within 300m
	8	Used for an item normally recorded
	9	Used for an item dealt with as misc inf
Yellow band		Delimits a defined published area within which an item has been found or located. This area should not be less than 25m square, nor greater than 250m square

Appendices

Conventional marking	Ex no	Significance of marking and notes on examples
	10	Used to show that somewhere in the banded area is the recorded item
Green cross		Marks the approximate centre of an area antiquity of unknown extent
	11	Used to locate a DMV,
Green band		Delimits the known extent of an area without linear boundaries. The inner edge is shaded in green if clarification is necessary
	12	Used to show an area of Roman mine-workings
	13	Used to indicate an area subject to misc inf

Bibliography

Chapter 2

Atkinson, R. J. C. *Field Archaeology*, 2nd ed (1953)
Cameron, K. *English Place Names* (1961)
Coles, J. *Field Archaeology in Britain* (1972)
Crawford, O. G. S. *Archaeology in the Field* (1953)
Fryer, D. H. *Surveying for Archaeologists*, 4th ed (University of Durham 1971)

Chapter 3

Beresford, M. W. *History on the Ground* (1957)
Harley, J. B. *Maps for the Local Historian* (1972)
Harley, J. B. and Phillips, C. W. *The Historian's Guide to Ordnance Survey Maps* (1964)

Chapter 4

Beresford, M. W. and St Joseph, J. K. S. *Medieval England: An Aerial Survey* (1958)
Bradford, J. *Ancient Landscapes* (1957)
Crawford, O. G. S. *Wessex from the Air* (1928)
RCAHM. *A Matter of Time – An Archaeological Survey of the River Gravels of England* (1960)
Riley, D. N. 'The Technique of Air-Archaeology', *Arch J*, C I (1944)
St Joseph, J. K. S. (ed). *The Uses of Air Photography* (1966)

Chapter 5

Benton, J. F. (ed). *Town Origins* (1968)

Carter, H. *The Towns of Wales* (1966)
Dyos, H. J. (ed). *The Study of Urban History* (1968)
Lobel, M. (ed). *Historic Towns Atlas*, vol I (1969)
Smailes, A. E. *The Geography of Towns* (1953)

Chapter 6

Beresford, M. W. and Hurst, J. G. *Deserted Medieval Villages* (1971)
Brunskill, R. W. *Illustrated Handbook of Vernacular Architecture* (1971)
Chisholm, M. *Rural Settlement and Land Use* (1962)
Cook, G. H. *The English Medieval Parish Church* (1954)
Finberg, J. *Exploring Villages* (1958)
Mills, D. R. *The English Village* (1968)
Sharp, T. *The Anatomy of the Village* (1946)

Chapter 7

Allcroft, A. H. *Earthwork of England* (1908)
Beresford and Hurst, op cit
Beresford and St Joseph, op cit
Beresford, M. W. *Lost Villages of England* (1954)

Chapter 8

Fowler, E. (ed). *Field Survey in British Archaeology* (1972)
Fowler, P. J. (ed). *Archaeology and the Landscape* (1972)

Acknowledgements

We would like to thank the following for their advice and encouragement: Don Benson, James Bond, John Hampton, Jim Pickering and Derek Riley. We would also like to express our thanks to Alison Smith for her continuous help with the text, to Shirley Baker for preparation of the figures and plates, and to Gabby Porter and Linda Rowley for the index.

We are grateful to the following for permission to reproduce photographs and other material in this volume:

Aerofilms for the plates on pages 35 and 86
BKS Surveys Ltd for the plate on page 85
Bodleian Library for the plate on page 171
Dr R. W. Brunskill for Appendix 3
Committee for Aerial Photography, Cambridge for the plates on pages 104, 153, 154, 171 and 172 (photographs by J. K. S. St Joseph, Cambridge University collection: copyright reserved)
Essex County Council, for Appendix 7
R. A. Foster for the plate on page 103
Ordnance Survey for Appendix 8
Oxford City and County Museum for Appendix 7
Royal Commission on Ancient and Historical Monuments for Fig 1 and for the plates on page 36 (Air Photographs Unit, National Monuments Record)
Monuments Record)

All other photographs and plans are the copyright of the authors

Index

Italic numerals indicate illustration pages

Abberwick, Northumb, *171*
Abbots Morton, Worcs, *150*
Abergavenny, 19
Abingdon, Oxon, 83, 114
Alchester, Oxon, 92
Aldwincles, Northants, 123
Allen, Major, 89
Almshouses, 114
Alnwick, Northumb, 111
Alvechurch, Worcs, 57, *58*
Arrow, River, *156*, 178-9
Ashbee, Paul, 19
Ashmolean Museum, Oxford, 88
Attington, Oxon, 174
Atcham, Salop, *63*
Aubrey, John, 16
Avon, River, *94*, 111

Banbury, Oxon, 115
Barford St John, shrunken settlement at, *142*
Barfords, Oxon, 123
Beaumaris Castle, 57
Beckley Park, Oxon, *158*
Bedfordshire, 70
Bell-pit mines, 161
Beverley (Fleming Gate), 115
Beresford, M. W., 15, 17, 94, 113, 141
Berkshire, 70: Downs, 13
Bicester, Oxon, 92, *98*, 110
Blanchland, Northumb, 126
Boarstall, Bucks, 66, *67*
Bobbington, Staffs, fishponds at, *152*
Bodinnar, Cornwall, *62*
Bordesley Abbey, Worcs, 155, *156*, 159, 178-9

211

Index

Bosvenning, Cornwall, *62*
Bridgetown Pomeroy, Devon, 79, 111
Brackley, Northants, 115
Bristol, 9, 79, *98*
Brunskill, R. W., building record cards, 52, 196
Buchanan Report, 90
Budbrooke, Warks, *152*
Burford, Oxon, *98*
Burgage plots, 99
Burhs, 102–7, 109: at Hereford, *100*; at Malmesbury, *94*; at Oxford and Wallingford, 101; at Totnes, 79
Burwell Castle, Camb, 21, *22*

Caernarvon, *108*
Cambridge: National Repository at, 70; University, Committee for Aerial Photography, 88
Canterbury, Kent, 99
Camden, William, 16
Cassington, Oxon, *38*
Castle Acre, Norfolk, 130, 140, *141*, *153*
Castle Camps, Camb, 133, *136*
Castle Pulverbatch, Salop, *120*
Castle Rising, Norfolk, *116*, 140, 149
Caus Castle, Salop, 94
Cemetery, 123: Saxon on M40, 174
Chester, 106, 114
Cheney Longville, Salop, *120*
Chichester, 102
Chipping Camden, Glos, 114
Chipping Norton, Oxon, *98*, 110
Chipping Ongar, Essex, 141
Church Brough, Westmorland, 146
Churches, 41, 52, 112, 114, 124–6, 133: Greyfriars, Oxford, 16; parish, 117, 122–4; plans of, 124–6, *125*
Churchill, Worcs, *150*
Cirencester, Glos, 93
Clare, Suffolk, 110, *141*
Claverdon, Warks, *163*
Cogges-by-Witney, Oxon, 115
Colchester, 102
Colt-Hoare, Sir Richard, 19
Congress of Archaeological Societies, Earthworks Committee, 20
Cornwall, parish survey, 170
Cotswolds: churches, 126; stone houses, 114
Council for British Archaeology, 20, 90
Crawford, O. G. S., 19, 18, 75, 88
Cricklade, Wilts, *85*, 102
Cropmarks, 13, 80–3, *78*, *87*

Deddington, Oxon, 115
Deserted medieval villages, 14, 16, 25, 39, 50, 66, 73, 79, 83, 127, 131, 143, *154*
Devizes, Wilts, 107

Index

Diocesan Records, 71
Domesday Book, 20, 57, 108
Dorchester-on-Thames, Oxon, 111
Dovecotes, 64, 119, 129
Drayton, Berks, *87*
Ducklington, Oxon, 133, *135*
Dugdale, Sir William, 16
Durham, *112*

Earthworks, 76–7, 79
East Layton, Co Durham, 66
East Tanfield, Yorks, 132
Ely, Camb, 110, *116*
Enclosure, Parliamentary, 15, 70–1, 143, 159–61: at Milton-under-Wychwood, *61*; of parkland, 157; roads terminated or diverted as result of, 127; West Cornwall, *62*
English Place-Name Society, 54
Essex, 70: County Council, 165; CC Archaeological Record, 205
Evesham, Worcs, 114
Eynsham, Oxon, *98*, 115, 170
Enstone, Oxon, 16, *134*, 143

Fallowfield, Northumb, 68
Feckenham, Worcs, 57, *58*, 60
Fishponds, 23, *40*, 64, 73, 133, 148, 149, *150*, 152, 155: at Alvechurch and Feckenham, 57, *58*; at Bordesley Abbey, *156*, 178–80; at Maxstoke Priory, Warks, *160*
Flint, *108*
Forest of Dean, medieval iron production in, 161
Fowler, Peter, 20
Fox, Sir Cyril, 50
Furnaces, 64

Gannow Green, Worcs, *150*
Gardens, 64, 164
Geoffrey of Monmouth, 15
Geology: drift, 31; maps, 31, 32
Giraldus Cambrensis, 15
Glass houses, 64
Glassmaking, 37, 64
Gloucester, 114
Goring Gap, 170
Gravels, 28: at Cassington, 38, 72; Upper Thames, 13
Greens, 121, 122, 128, 140
Grinsell, Leslie, 19

Halesowen, Worcs, 68
Halton, Northumb, *154*
Hamilton, Leics, deserted village at, 132
Hanbury, 148
Harley, J. B., 69, 72
Haughley, Suffolk, 141
Haverfordwest, *93*, 107
Heath, Salop, 125, 157

213

Index

Hedges, 14, 26, 72, 144: dating of, 161
Hen Domen, Montgomery, 77, 133
Hereford, 99, *100*: defences, 106; market, 110, 113
Hexham, Northumb, 126
Holloways, 127, 137, 163
Hooper, Dr Max, 161
Hoskins, W. G., 15, 17, 119

Ipswich, 106

Kenilworth Castle, 146, *147*
Kent, Weald of, 161
Kent, William, 64
Kilns, pottery, 34, 64, 162
Kilpeck, 21, *22*, 107

Lancashire, 70
Lanhydrock Atlas, 62
Lavenham, Suffolk, 113
Lechlade, Gloucs, 170
Leicester, 106, 115
Leland, John, 16
Lewknor, Oxon, 142, 174
Lincoln, 97, *98*, 99, 115
Liverpool, *93*, 97
London, 115: National Repository at, 70
Lower Dornford, Oxon, 137, *138*
Ludlow, Salop, *86*, 111, 115
Lynchets, 64, 145

M40, 142, *176*: Archaeological Research Group, 170, 173–5
Malmesbury, Wilts, *94*
Malvern, Worcs, 126
Maps, 56–74: county, 59–60; enclosure, 61, 70–1; OS, 59, 60, 68, 69, 71–4, 83, 165–6, 168; Speed's, 69; tithe, 61, 28, 29, *58*, 70–1, 148, 173; town maps and plans, 63, 69, 96, 97, *98*, 99, *100*, *101*, 102
Markets, 109, 110, 115, 146
Marl pits, 39, 66
Marlborough, Wilts, 110
Marsh Baldon, Oxon, *121*
Maxstoke Priory, Warks, 159, *160*
Medieval Village Research Group, 54, 131, 139: questionnaire, 198
Merton church, Oxon, *104*
Middleton Stoney, Oxon, *18*, 64: park, *158*
Midhurst, Sussex, 57
Midlands: deserted medieval villages, 39, 133; field boundaries, 159–60; fishponds, 152; moated sites, 149, *150*; ridge and furrow, 144
Mills, 24, 32, 57, 62, 64, 66, 73, 148, 149, 155
Milton-under-Wychwood, Oxon, *61*
Minster Lovell, Oxon, 124
Moated Sites Research Group, 54, 149, 201
Moats, 25: at Alvechurch, 57, *58*; at Ducklington, 133, *135*; in Midlands, *150*; moated

214

Index

farmsteads, 133, 146–9; moated lodges, 135; moated manors, 119, *160*; moated sites, *158*, *163*; moated villages, 73
Monasteries: enclosures, 123; granges, 129; precinct, 126; sites, 14, 26, 37, 114, 128, 139, 159
Monuments, archaeological, 16, 19, 21
Morton Bagot, Warks, *150*
Motte and bailey castles, *18*, 57, *95*, 107–8, 119, 145

National Datum, 48
National Farmers Union, 29
National Grid, 47, 60, 74, 88, 137, 168, 169
National Library of Wales, 71
National Monuments Record, 84, 88, 167, 169, 174, 180
Nettles, 139
Newbridge, Cornwall, *62*
Newport, Salop, 109
Newton Purcell, Oxon, shrunken settlement at, *142*
North of England: industrial housing in, 52; deserted medieval villages, 39
Northampton, Hampshire, 99, *102*, 106, 115
Northamptonshire, 70, 123, 141
Norwich, 106
Nottingham, 99
Nuneham Courtenay, Oxon, *121*

Offa's Dyke, 50, 158
Old Radnor, Radnorshire, *104*, 119
Old Sarum, Wilts, 16, *17*
Ordnance Survey, Archaeology Division, 19–20, 73, 75, 88, 167, 168, 169, 180: benchmarks, 48; conventions, 206; maps for Institute of Geological Sciences, 31; publications dept, 74
Orford, Suffolk, 141
Ottery St Mary, Devon, 115
Oxford: Ashmolean Museum, 88; castle, 107, 108; defences, 106; Greyfriars Church, 16; market, 109; National Repository at, 70; Oxford City and County Museum, 88, 165, 173; Primary Record Card from, 167, 204; recording sites around, 166; recording sites in, 168; sites and monuments record, 166–70; town plan, 99, *101*
Oxford University: Department for External Studies, 173; Research Lab for Art and Archaeology, 174
Oxfordshire, 32, 123: deserted medieval villages in, 133; local fieldworkers in, 167; medieval towns of, 97, *98*; shrunken villages in, *142*; *VCH* plans of, 69

Parliamentary enclosure, 15
Pershore, Worcs, 115, 126
Philips, C. W., 72
Pleshey, Essex, 107
Plot, Robert, 16
Pontefract, Yorks, 106, 115, *116*
Postcombe, Oxon, 174
Public Record Office, 71

Quarrendon, Bucks, deserted village at, 132

Index

Raybridge, Essex, 141
Redditch New Town, Worcs, 155, 175: recording sites in, 175, *177*
Richard's Castle, 94, *95*, 107
Richmond, Yorks, 107
Ridge and furrow, 15, *18*, 24, *36*, 37, 66, 77, 82, 137, 139, 143–4, 145: at Ducklington, *135*; at Halton, *154*; at Stratford-upon-Avon and Thame, *105*; at Wormleighton, 137, *138*; characteristic medieval, 99, 144, *171*
Riley, D., 89
Rock, Worcs, 125
Rocque, John, 59
Roskennal, Cornwall, *62*
Rousham, Oxon, 64, *65*
Royal Commission on Ancient and Historic Monuments, 20–1, 84, 145, 180: volumes published, 195
Roofs, 32, 34, 53, 129, 130

St Joseph, Prof J. K. S., 19, 88
St Kenelm, 124
Salford, Oxon, *163*
Saltings, 66, 162
Sawley Abbey, W. Riding, 159, *172*
Seacourt, Berks, 50
Severn, River, 111
Shrewsbury, Salop, 92, 106, 108, 115
Shropshire, castle settlements in, *120*
Skelton, R. A., 60
Somerton, Oxon: castle at, 167, *203*; shrunken village at, 142, *171*
Sopwith, Staffs, *47*
Southampton, *102*, 106, 115
Speed, John, 59, 69
Standlake, Oxon, 170
Stanton Harcourt, 170
Stoke Mandeville, Bucks, deserted village at, 132
Stoke St Milborough, Salop, 125
Stokenchurch, Oxon, 142, 173
Stratford-upon-Avon, 99, *105*, 115
Stukeley, William, 16
Sussex, West, 70, 161

Tackley, Oxon, *163*
Tamworth, Staffs, 116
Tanworth, Warks, 149, *151*: Botley Mill at, *152*; Ladbroke Park, *158*
Tardebigge, Worcs, Weights Farm, *152*
Tate, W. E., 71
Taylor, Isaac, 59
Telford, Thomas, 19
Tetsworth, Oxon, 142, 174
Tewkesbury, Glos, 126
Thame, Oxon, 99, *105*, 110, 142
Tithe barns, 119, 129
Tonbridge, Kent, 107
Toot Baldon, Oxon, shrunken settlement at, *142*

Totnes, Devon, *35*, 79, 111
Towns: deserted, 140–1; at Castle Acre and Clare, *141*; planted, 15, 92, 96–9, 102, 111

Ullenhall, Warks, 149, *151*
Upper Thames Valley, 13, 89, 170

Victoria County Histories, 20, 56, 69, 145, 169: published volumes, 194
Villages: planted, 121–2, *121*; shrunken, 141–3, *142*, *171*
Vineyards, 64

Wales: castles, 145; monastic enclosures in, 123; National Library of, 71; RCAHM for, 20
Wallingford, Berks, *101*, 102, 106, 107, 109
Wantage, Berks, *103*
Wareham, Dorset, 102, 107
Warwick, 95, *96*, *103*, 106, 107, 109, 111, 113, 116
Warwickshire, south, deserted medieval villages in, 133, *134*
Washford, Worcs, 39, *40*, 155
Waterstock, Oxon, 42, 173
Wells Cathedral, 112
Welsh marches, 94, 107, 140: defensive considerations in, 119; failed towns in, 92; motte and bailey castles in, 145
West Felton, Salop, *120*
West of England, monastic enclosures in, 123
Westminster, 115
Wharram Percy, E. Riding, Yorks, 50, 132
Whitchurch, Salop, 115
William of Malmesbury, 16
William of Worcester, 16
Wiltshire, 69
Winchester, Statute of (1285), 109
Witney, Oxon, *98*
Wood, Eric S., 20
Woodstock, Oxon, *98*, 110: park at, 157, *158*
Worcester, 11, *112*: Greyfriars, 112
Wormleighton, Warks, 137, *138*
Wroxeter, 92
Wymondham, Norfolk, 126

Yeavering, Northumb, 82
York, 106